David Philipson

Old European Jewries

David Philipson

Old European Jewries

ISBN/EAN: 9783337138219

Printed in Europe, USA, Canada, Australia, Japan

Cover: Foto ©ninafisch / pixelio.de

More available books at **www.hansebooks.com**

OLD EUROPEAN JEWRIES

BY

DAVID PHILIPSON, D. D.

AUTHOR OF "THE JEW IN ENGLISH FICTION," ETC.

"By the Ghetto's plague,
By the garb's disgrace"
BROWNING

PHILADELPHIA
THE JEWISH PUBLICATION SOCIETY
OF AMERICA

TO MY WIFE,

WHO, WITH SYMPATHETIC INTEREST, VISITED
WITH ME MANY OF THE PLACES
HEREIN MENTIONED,
THIS BOOK IS LOVINGLY INSCRIBED.

PREFACE.

When, several years ago, I planned a trip abroad, one of my objects was to visit the remains of the old Jewish quarters in some of the European cities. Before that time, I had determined to write the story of the Ghetto, and it occurred to me that it would add interest to the work if I could supplement my studies by a view of the sites of certain old Jewries. This I found to be the case, for memories linger about these spots which bring their history vividly to mind.

I have limited myself to a study of the officially instituted Ghetto. The legislation restricting Jews in the choice of their dwelling places was in a line with the general policy of church and state towards them up to this century. At

(1)

times, it is true, Jews resided together in separate portions of cities even when they were not forced to do so by law. For the formation of these voluntary Ghettos there were various reasons, which I point out in one of the chapters of this book.

I have included a chapter on the Russian Pale of Settlement, the great modern Ghetto, because it is germane to the subject. We see the evils and horrors of the old Ghetto repeated in our own day in these districts.

We can not but stand amazed at the endurance of the Jew which enabled him to triumph over the nameless woes which the thought of the Ghetto suggests. It is one of the wonders of history.

CINCINNATI, *July*, 1894.

CONTENTS.

CHAPTER I.

After the destruction of Jerusalem by
the Romans in the year 70 C. E., the Jews
cast about for new dwelling places. Long
before this event Jews had settled in
the various capitals of the then civilized
world, in Alexandria, Antioch, Rome, the
cities of Asia Minor and Egypt. In Rome,
the influence of their religious teachings
became apparent as early as 76 B. C. E.,[1]
but their settlement in considerable numbers is usually dated from the time of
Pompey, the first Roman general to enter
Jerusalem and carry Jews to Rome;[2]
thereafter, the Jewish colony received ad-
ditions from time to time. Outside of
Rome, it is not likely that there were
Jewish settlements in western Europe before the beginning of the Christian era,
although there were traditions current in

later days among the Jews themselves that
some of their number had settled in portions of Europe in very early times. For
example, it has been asserted that there
were synagogues in Germany, at Ulm and
Worms, before the origin of Christianity.
The Spanish Jews had a tradition that
there were Jews in Spain as early as the
days of King Solomon.[3]   But these pre-
tensions cannot be established, and will
not bear scrutiny.   The earliest authentic
notices concerning the Jews in European
lands date from the first Christian centuries.   Titus, the conqueror of Jerusalem,
we know, deported thousands of Jewish
captives to the western Roman provinces.
Many were sent to Sardinia to work in
the mines, many remained in Rome, and
we have frequent notices of them during
the reigns of succeeding emperors.   Into
the Italian cities, they naturally drifted
from Rome.   As for Spain, the earliest authentic notice is by the apostle Paul, who,
in his Epistle to the Romans, says :
" Whensoever I take my journey into
Spain, I will come to you ; for I trust to

see you in my journey, and to be brought
on my way thitherward by you ; "[4] and " I
will come by you into Spain."[5] Paul, we
know, journeyed only to places in which
Jews dwelt, or in which Jewish teachings had been established, for only those
acquainted with Jewish doctrines could
understand him. At any rate, Jews dwelt
in Spain before the beginning of the fourth
century, for the council of Illiberis, held
in 305, devoted four decrees to the Jews,
forbidding the Christians to live on intimate terms with them, this showing that
there must have been a considerable number of Jews living in Spain at that time.
Among these paragraphs are the following : If heretics are unwilling to join the
Catholic Church, Catholic girls must not
be given to them in marriage ; but neither
to Jews nor to heretics should they be
given, because there can be no association for the faithful with the unbeliever.
If parents act contrary to this prohibition,
they shall be cut off from communion for
five years.[6]

If, then, any ecclesiastic or any of the

faithful partakes of food with Jews, he
shall be deprived of communion, so that
this may be corrected.[7]

Owners (of land) are warned not to
permit their products which they receive
from God to be blessed by Jews, lest they
make our blessing useless and weak. If
anyone shall presume to do this after this
prohibition, he shall be excluded from the
church.[8]

These decrees definitely prove that there
were Jews in Spain as early as 300.

As for France, or Gaul, as the province
was called in early days, it is unknown,
according to Graetz, when the Jews first
settled there.[9] There is no proof of
their residence prior to the second century.

Depping,[10] arguing from the expressions
of Constantine regarding the Jews of Cologne, concludes that they may have been
dwelling in some of the cities of north-
western Europe before the attention of
the Roman emperors was directed to them.
In a law of the Theodosian code[11] (com-
piled between 425 and 435), addressed to

the prefect of Gaul, a favorable mention of the Jews occurs, which would go to prove that they were then firmly settled, and were scattered throughout Gaul and Belgium.

According to tradition, Jews settled in Germany in hoary antiquity. When, in the time of the crusades, the Jews of western Europe were held responsible for the death of Jesus, and thousands upon thousands of them were slaughtered by the wild mobs on that account, some tale had to be invented to disprove the charge, and the Jews put forth the claim that they had had a congregation in Worms long before the time of Jesus, in fact, as early as the days of Ezra, and that, therefore, they were not concerned with nor responsible for the crucifixion. According to another tradition, the Jews of southern Germany were descendants of the soldiers who had sacked Jerusalem. These soldiers, the Van-giones—so ran the story—had selected beautiful Jewish women as their portion of the spoil, carried them to their quarters on the Rhine and the Main, and there consorted with them. Their children were

reared as Jews by their mothers, and were
the founders of the Jewish communities
between Worms and Mayence.[12] This,
however, is all legendary. The earliest reli-
able notices of the settlement of Jews in
German cities inform us that there were
Jews in Cologne in the fourth century,[13] in
Magdeburg, Merseburg[14] and Ratisbon[15] in
the tenth, and in Mayence, Speyer, Worms
and Treves[16] in the eleventh. As for Nuremberg, one chronicler states that Jews
dwelt there in the year 100, another makes
it as early as 46, but historical data do not
justify us in considering their residence
there as assured before the time of Emperor Henry IV in the eleventh century.[17]
Undoubtedly, Jews did dwell in the German cities before the tenth and eleventh
centuries, for in those times they were
present in large numbers, but no earlier
archives and authentic documents mention
them.

As for the Jews in England, the first
notices we have of their presence in that
country before the Norman conquest are
in the collections of canon laws made by

Theodorus, Archbishop of Canterbury, and Egbert, Archbishop of York, for the regulation of the church. By these laws the Jews are subjected to much the same prohibitions as those formulated by the church councils. Theodorus was archbishop from 669 to 691, and Egbert, from 735 to 766.[18] There is one more notice of the residence of Jews in England in early days. A document issued by King Witglaff, of Mercia, in 833, confirms the right of the monks of the cloister of Croyland to all the possessions given them by earlier kings of Mercia, nobles and other faithful Christians, and also to those received from Jews as gift, pledge or otherwise.[19]

All argument as to the earlier residence of Jews in these lands is necessarily conjectural ; it seems justifiable to conclude that they settled wherever a home was offered them, but until positive proofs are produced to the contrary, we must regard those given above as the earliest authentic notices. The first settlements of Jews in European lands are still shrouded in mystery.[20]

Up to the time of the crusades the condition of the Jews in Europe was bearable. There were outbursts of the persecuting spirit now and then, notably in the reigns of the Visigothic kings in Spain and the Merovingian in France ; there were bitter attacks made against them by churchmen, such as Amolo and Agobard, of Lyons ; but compared with the fiendish treatment inaugurated by the mobs on their way to Palestine to conquer the sepulcher of their Lord, the life of the Jews during the first ten Christian centuries was almost blissful. They were free citizens, could dwell wherever they liked, and were on terms of friendship and intimacy with the Christian population. If they had not been, decrees would not have been passed by the church councils forbidding such intimacy. They followed what pursuits they pleased, and on the whole led peaceful lives. But with the fanatical cry resounding throughout Europe at the time of the crusades : " Exterminate the enemies of Christ at home before fighting against them in the far East," the terrible woes of the Jews began, and the bloody chapter of the persecutions of centuries was opened. The Jew was safe nowhere in France, Germany, England and Austria, the countries especially affected by the crusades. The mobs, incited by the priesthood, robbed, plundered, outraged, murdered, exterminated. In those dark times, to protect the Jews as far as possible from the persecutions of the populace and the venom of the priesthood, and to assure their right of residence in the different cities and districts, the emperors of the Holy Roman Empire and the kings of various countries took them under their special protection, for pecuniary considerations, of course, and the Jews became the so-called *servi cameræ*, servants of the chamber, of the emperor or king. The idea gained ground that the Jews were subject to the emperor directly, were to be protected by him everywhere, and had to pay for this protection. This servitude did not mean that they were slaves or serfs, with whose life or goods the emperor or king could do as he pleased, but merely that they had to pay tribute for his protection. In the end it virtually robbed them of their freedom, since these rulers did with them much as they wished. The exact date of the beginning of this relation cannot be determined. The emperors pleased themselves with the fiction that this subjection and protection began with the taking of Jerusalem by Titus; that the Jews came under the protection of the Roman emperors at that time, and that, as they were the legitimate successors of the emperors of Rome, they acquired the rights of the latter. This contention is not worthy of serious consideration. The servitude of the chamber was a new institution, called forth by the terrible calamities that befell the Jews, and was at the time welcomed as a boon, as almost anything would have been that promised respite and deliverance. Graetz[21] says that in Germany this protection was systematically instituted in the reign of Frederick Barbarossa. Henry IV protected them in 1103. Conrad III, during the second crusade, gave the Jews who applied to him for protection refuge in Nuremberg. Although there are these instances of protection in the twelfth, yet according to Stobbe[22] it was only in the thirteenth century that the institution of *servi cameræ* was established. In the reign of Frederick II,[22] the Jews are called special servants of the chamber, and in 1246 Conrad IV calls the Jews of Frankfort *servi cameræ nostræ*.

In France and England,[23] a like relation was supposed to hold between the Jews and the kings. This supposition of the special jurisdiction of the emperor or king over the Jews exerted a great influence upon their residence in various cities and districts. Jews were looked upon in one light only, viz., as a source of revenue. For example, in 1407, Emperor Rupert commanded that the Jews be not too heavily burdened, lest they be forced to emigrate, and the cities so suffer a diminution of income ; in 1480, Frederick III commanded that the Jews of Ratisbon be treated in such a manner that they might restore their fortunes in five years to an extent sufficient to enable them to pay the emperor 10,000 gulden. As they were so

great a source of income, the emperor,
when in need, often sold the Jews of a city
to princes, counts or bishops for a stipu-
lated sum, with the understanding that
thereafter the purchaser was to enjoy the
income derived from taxing them. He
sometimes even sold the right to parties
not connected with the government of
the cities in which the Jews lived. For
instance, in 1263, the Jews of Worms
were turned over to the jurisdiction of the
bishop of Speyer; in 1279, the Jews of
the dioceses of Strasburg and Basle, to
the bishop of Basle.[24]

Often, if the emperor owed money to
some ruler or bishop, he gave the Jews
over to him for a number of years, until
taxes equal to the debt were collected; or,
if he was in need of money, he borrowed
it on the same security; and if a ruler,
noble or priest was in debt to the citizens,
he did the same. The archbishop of
Mayence was in debt to the citizens of Erfurt; his income from the Jews of Erfurt,
whose protection or, in other words, the
right to tax whom, had been transferred

to him by the emperor, was 100 marks a
year ; this income he granted the citizens
of the city for four years. The emperors
also often sold to cities the rights over the
Jews. It was the most convenient manner
of raising money. It can be well understood how all this affected the residence
of the Jews in the cities. They were
granted the right to dwell there, because
they were sources of revenue. Otherwise
they would not have been tolerated long.

The right of residence in places in which
they had not yet dwelt was also a privilege
sold or granted by the emperor. It was,
indeed, a privilege for a ruler to have Jews
in his domain, for it meant a certain income, and as princes were always in need
of money, this permission to have Jews
was much sought for. The technical term
for this permission was *Judæos tenere*,[25]
or *Judæos habere*, the right to keep or to
have Jews. It can be seen how precarious
their residence everywhere was ; they had
the right to dwell not as men, but as taxable property on a footing with all other
sources of income. They had to pay for

2

the mere privilege of living, and even then
had not the freedom to choose their dwelling place. For the most part, a special
quarter was assigned to them.

The conditions of their residence having
been discussed, the consideration of the
place of dwelling granted them by their
masters, the rulers and the peoples of
European lands, may now be turned to.

CHAPTER II.

THE INSTITUTION OF THE GHETTO.

Every possible method to degrade and
harass the Jews, and mark them off from the
remainder of the population was invented
and employed in the dark, mediæval days.
Decrees innumerable, regulating the life of
the Jews and their intercourse with Christians, were passed at church council upon
church council, and incorporated into the
canon law, and often into civil legislation.
Laws prohibiting them to hold offices, to
eat or associate with Christians, to employ
Christian nurses or servants, to appear on
the streets during Passion Week, and many
more of the same kind, were enacted time
and again. But all such prohibitions, irri-
tating and troublesome as they were, were
yet naught compared with two regulations
which only fiendish ingenuity could have
invented to crush unfortunates whose only
crime lay in the fact that the faith they

confessed was a reproach to the claims of
Christianity. One was the device proposed
by Pope Innocent III, decreed by the
Fourth Lateran Council in 1215, and
thereupon by every church council of that
century convened anywhere in Europe—
from Oxford in England, in 1222, to Buda
in Hungary, in 1279—compelling every
Jew to wear on his clothes a mark, usually
a piece of yellow cloth, by which he might
be at once known as a Jew. From that
time on the Jew was a marked creature.
The command was received by the unfortunates with a wail of despair resounding
throughout Europe. Effort upon effort
was made to have it revoked or to evade it,
but all in vain. It was the will of the church,
and the Jew had to submit. The other
device adopted to completely isolate the
Jews was to shut them up in separate quarters, originally called *vicus Judæorum*,
later known as *Judengasse, Judenstrasse* or
Judenviertel in Germany, as *Ghetto* in
Italy, as *Judiaria* in Portugal, as *Juiverie*
in France, as *Carriera* in Provence and
Comtat Venaissin. Here, penned up like

cattle, they were to live apart from the Christians. This systematic exclusion began with the fourteenth century. Before that time Jews had inhabited quarters by themselves, but from choice, not because they had been forced into them.

What a picture the Ghetto recalls ! The narrow, gloomy streets, with the houses towering high on either side ; the sunlight rarely streaming in ; situated in the worst slums of the city ; shut off by gates barred and bolted every night with chains and locks, none permitted to enter or depart from sundown to sunrise ! The solution had at last been found ; the Jew was effectually excluded. The Christian no longer would be corrupted and contaminated by the close proximity of the followers of the *superstitio et perfidia Judaica*, "the Jewish superstition and perfidy." For four centuries this lasted. As we to-day remove the victims of a pestilence far away from the inhabited portions of our cities, from fear of contagion, so the Jews were cut off by the walls of the Ghetto as though stricken with some loathsome disease that might carry misery and death unto others if they lived in close contact with them. The Ghetto has been well stigmatized as a "pest-like isolation."[26] Speaking of the sixteenth century one writer says : " Stone walls arose in all places wherein Jews dwelt, shutting off their quarters like pesthouses ; the Ghetto had become epidemic."[27]

At first, as was said above, this dwelling in separate quarters was not compulsory; the Jews lived together in their own quarters before hostile legislation forced them into the Ghettos. For this we can assign several reasons. One was their fear of the remainder of the population, and another their *esprit de corps*. They naturally felt that if they lived together, they could assist one another better in case of need. In some instances, in fact, it was considered a favor when the temporal or ecclesiastical ruler of a city assigned them a quarter in which they would be protected, as Bishop Rüdiger of Speyer did in 1084.[28] According to some historians,[29] their inhabiting separate quarters was due to the fact that in mediæval times people of the same industrial, social or commercial class were accustomed to dwell together in certain streets, and the Jews, forming a separate community whose center was the synagogue, naturally lived together. Whatever truth there may be in this contention (and the strong feeling of a common religion and a common past did hold the Jews together), there can be no doubt that the authorities later enclosed them in separate quarters to disgrace them and prevent their having too intimate relations with the Christians. Such is the reason given in the decrees, quoted in a subsequent chapter, ordering their dwelling in separate quarters.

The names applied to these Jewish quarters in different countries, noted above, are readily explained, with the exception of the one now commonly adopted in all languages to designate the isolation of the Jews in Christian communities, viz., the word *Ghetto*. There have been various explanations of the word. Its form points to Italian origin, and in truth, it was first

used of the Jewish quarters in Italian cities.
Italian Jews derived the word, which they
spelled *g-u-c-t-o*, from the Hebrew word
get, " bill of divorce," finding the idea of
divorce expressed by the one term, and
that of exclusion in the other, sufficiently
analagous to point to a common origin.
Another explanation connects the word
Ghetto with the German *Gitter*, " bars."[30]
This suggestion has not much in its favor.
That the Ghetto resembled nothing so
much as a barred cage is true enough, but
a likeness of this kind is not sufficient to
found an etymological explanation upon.
Still another and more plausible explanation has been offered for the origin of the
word. It is traced to Venice, in which a separate Jewish quarter existed in 1516. The
Jewish quarter was called Ghetto, because
it lay in the vicinity of a cannon foundry,
which in Italian is termed *gheta*.[31] This
designation, belonging first only to the
Venetian Jewry, soon became general.
Berliner adduces, as an example of simi-
larly wide application of a special term derived from a particular locality, the word

catacombs, the name of the subterranean burial vaults of Rome, derived from the first burial place of the kind, which was situated *ad Catacombas.* I may also mention the suggestion that the word is an abbreviation of the Italian *borghetto*, small burg or quarter.[32]

The fifteenth century may be set as the time in which the Ghetto was established as the legal dwelling place of the Jews. As mentioned above, before that time they had dwelt apart, but the isolation was optional, at times sought as a privilege. But from the fifteenth century on, Ghettos became general ; in almost every city in which Jews dwelt, a Ghetto was formed. In the next chapter will be given some ecclesiastical legislation on the subject. At present, it will suffice to take a rapid survey of the European lands, to see how general the Ghettos were. Comparatively few of the cities will be mentioned, for, as one, so all.

In Portugal, even before the fifteenth century, in all cities and places in which over ten Jews lived, there was a separate

Jewish quarter, known as *Judiaria.* In Lisbon, the chief city, there were several Judiarias, and in all other cities Jewish quarters existed. These Judiarias were closed every evening when the bells sounded for prayer, and were guarded by two watchmen appointed by the king. Any Jew found outside of the Judiaria after the first three tollings of the bells was fined ten liveres, or, according to an order of King Dom Pedro, was whipped through the city, and in case of repetition of the offense, punished with confiscation of his property. These laws being so stringent, the Jews petitioned for their amelioration. King João I promised to lighten their burden, and in 1412 issued new regulations. According to these, every Jew over fifteen years of age found outside the Judiaria after the given signal, was fined for the first offense five thousand liveres, for the second ten thousand, and for the third was publicly whipped. These laws were made bearable by favorable exceptions. For example, if a Jew, returning from a distant point, was

delayed beyond the given hour, he was
not subjected to punishment ; he was
merely compelled to take the shortest way
to the Judiaria, and in case it was closed,
he could spend the night elsewhere.[33]

In Italy the first Ghetto in which the
Jews were forced to live was established
in Venice, in March, 1516,[34] on the island
Lunga Spina. The celebrated Ghetto of
Rome, possibly the worst and most noisome
of all, was established in 1556, by Pope
Paul IV Caraffa, of evil memory among
Jews.[35] With this precedent, the Ghetto
became a common institution. The other
Italian cities quickly followed, Turin, Flor-
ence, Pisa, Ferrara,[36] Genoa,[37] Mantua,[38]
Beneventum[39] and Naples.[40]

In Sicily the Jews were placed in separate quarters, long before it was done in
the Italian cities. In 1312, Frederick II
ordered that the Jews of Palermo should
live apart from the Christians, in fact, outside of the city walls ; they were, however,
soon after permitted to occupy a quarter
within the city,[41] in the vicinity of the
town hall and the Augustinian cloister.

The Moschita Court adjoining contained
the synagogue, a hospital and forty-four
dwellings.[42]

In 1392, the monk Julian obtained permission, as royal commissioner, to drive
all Sicilian Jews into Ghettos.[43] In Tra-
pani, the Jewish quarter lay next to the
city wall. When this needed repairs, the
citizens wished to put the burden of the
repairs upon the Jewish community, but
the government compelled all to share in
the expense.[44] In Castro a special officer,
mentioned in a document of the year 1416,
had jurisdiction over the Ghetto.[45]

In Germany, the freedom of the Jews
began to be impaired in the middle of the
twelfth century, the time at which their
residence outside of Jewish quarters was
first forbidden.[46] In Cologne they were
compelled to live in their own quarter as
early as this. A *porta Judæorum*, "Jews'
gate," is mentioned in 1206, a *propugna-
culum Judæorum*, "Jews' bulwark," in 1246.
According to the Cologne city records of
the year 1341, the town officer was to have
the keys of the Jews' gates ; he was to lock

the gates at sundown, and unlock them at prime, for which service the Jews had to pay him twenty marks yearly.[47] The Jews of Ratisbon lived in the *Judenviertel*,[48] separated from the rest of the city by three large and three small gates, locked every evening and opened every morning. In Nuremberg, in 1349, a special quarter was assigned to them, and when their numbers had greatly increased, the authorities were forced to name certain other streets in which they might acquire property.[49] In 1460, the Jews of Frankfort were forced to leave their dwellings in all portions of the city, and live in one assigned street.[50] Most German cities had their *Judengasse*. In Ueberlingen, the street in which the Jews lived was so designated. A *porta Judæorum* in Worms is mentioned in 1231. To keep stricter watch over the doings of the Jews, the archbishop of Treves, in conjuction with the civic authorities, concluded in 1362 that the Jews should have but three gates leading into the streets of the city, and that the rest of the gates should be walled up. In some cities, the brothels

were transferred to the *Judengasse*, this
being regarded as of ill repute. In 1375,
the council of Schweidnitz, in answer to
a petition of the Jews, promised that no
fallen women should thereafter be transferred to their street.[51] A recent writer
mentions two Jewish gravestones of the
year 1379 in Rothenburg an der Tauber
as reminding him of the days when the
Jews all dwelt in the *Gasse*.[52] The Jewish
quarter of Speyer dates from the year
1084.[53] At first granted as a privilege, it,
too, became the enforced dwelling place
of the unfortunate people. So throughout
Germany, Austria, Bohemia and Eastern
lands, the *Gasse* became an established
institution. Karl Emil Franzos speaks of
the Ghetto of his native town as an "out-
cast quarter, which stretches along the unhealthy morasses of the river of our town.
Pestilential vapors poison the atmosphere,
which remains gloomy in spite of the
clearest sunshine."

The private houses of the Ghettos, notably in the larger cities, were high and
narrow, and harbored several families.

However much the Jews' quarters in different localities may have varied in appearance, two homes were common to them all, the synagogue and "the home of the dead." The synagogue was naturally the center of the communal life of the Jews; their religion was the bond that joined them. In the synagogue, they assembled every day for service, and in prayer there, they gained the strength and endurance necessary to live their lives. Their religion was an integral portion of their existence, and dominated its every hour. Their God was ever in their thoughts, and very near unto them. Their religion was truly their life. And that other spot found in every Ghetto, that last home of the mortal frame, too often was the only resting place they could hope for. In the Ghetto, it was called the "good place," and who knows unto how many, during the sad days marked by fanaticism, it appeared as a good place, better than any other earthly habitation. Usually situated at the end of the *Gasse*, the cemetery was a common feature of all Jewish quarters.

The Jews found rest in the synagogue and in the burying ground; the one was the emblem of the living faith, the undying bond that joined the Jews all over the earth; the other, the eternal home of the generations that had been steadfast to the faith of the fathers, and had been filled with the hope of a better and brighter future, in which the time of suffering would be fulfilled, and their God would bring peace and rest to His people, was the symbol of fealty in death to the same faith. In a measure, that time of surcease of suffering has come. The Jews in the civilized world are as free as other men. God has brought liberty and freedom to them. May the myriads who lived, suffered, prayed, endured, hoped, and died in exclusion, rest in peace! Their descendants are enjoying the benefits of that better day which they felt sure that the God of mercy would bring about, as they expressed it, "in His own time."

There was one other communal house in some Jewish quarters, which should be referred to. Sad as was their position,

the Ghetto Jews had their joys and pleas-
ures, not only in the family circle, but also
in their communal life. It must not be
imagined that they continually lived in
the shadow of exclusion. It was not con-
stantly present to their thoughts. Years
and centuries accustomed them to their
life, and the natural buoyancy of human
creatures is bound to assert itself. There
were not always active persecutions, and
in quiet times, the life of the inhabitants
of the Ghetto flowed along much as
life elsewhere does, with its joy and
sorrow, its happiness and woe, its pleasure
and grief. For the joyous element, provision was made in what was known as
the " Dance house." The larger communities, such as those at Frankfort,
Eger, Augsburg, Rothenburg, etc., had
their own dance houses, which, besides
serving the purpose indicated by their
name, when necessary, may have been
used as gathering places for more earnest
occasions. " Here the Jewish girls could
appear without the two blue stripes on
their veils, and the men without the dis-

tinguishing mark on their clothes or the
peaked hat on their heads."[54]   It is grati-
fying to think that there were bright
spots, too, in that long life of misery,
separation and exclusion.   The very fact
that the Jews outlived the depression and
the evils of the cramped Ghetto existence,
and retained the elasticity of temperament
which still marks them, speaks volumes
for the optimism with which their faith
imbued them.   Not all the wrongs and
ills of centuries could crush the spirit of
hope that had its well-springs in the words
of their prophets.   A trustful earnestness
marked them, and tided them over the
evil times.   The evil times that invented
the Ghetto are, it is to be hoped, gone
forever; the present, in western Europe
and in America, at least, is bright with
the promise of better things.   In the cities
of the western and southern European
lands, "the Ghetto doors have been removed; the Jew is no longer cooped up
in the worst slums of the city, and separated from his fellow townsmen by gates
and chains."

CHAPTER III.

THE GHETTO IN CHURCH LEGISLA-
TION.

In order that the various motives that
led to the establishment of the Ghetto or
Jewish quarter may be better understood,
some of the original acts of church authorities, and councils ordering the dwelling
apart of Jews, and stating the reasons
therefor will be given here.

Reference has been made several times
in the foregoing pages to the act of Rüdiger, Bishop of Speyer, by which, in the
year 1084, he conferred upon the Jews of
his diocese what were then considered
privileges. He assigned them a separate
portion of the city surrounded by a wall,
gave them their own burying ground,
granted them jurisdiction in their own
affairs, etc. This was before the days in
which the Ghetto was instituted as a mark
of disgrace, but the document[55] is interesting from the fact that it is the oldest

extant dealing with a distinctly Jewish quarter.

" In the name of the holy and indivisible Trinity, when I, Rüdiger, also called Huozmann, Bishop of Speyer, changed the town of Speyer into a city, I thought that I would add to the honor of our place by bringing in Jews. Accordingly, I located them outside of the community and habitation of the other citizens, and that they might not readily be disturbed by the insolence of the populace, I surrounded them with a wall. Their place of habitation I had acquired in a just manner; the hill partly with money, partly by exchange; the valley I had received from (some) heirs as a gift. That place, I say, I gave over to them on the condition that they would pay three pounds and a half of the money of Speyer annually for the use of the (monastery) brothers. Within their dwelling place and outside thereof, up to the harbor of the ships, and in the harbor itself, I granted them full permission to change gold and silver; to buy and sell anything

they pleased, and that same permission I
gave them throughout the state. In addition, I gave them out of the property of
the church a burial place with hereditary
rights. I also granted the following
rights : If any stranger Jew lodge with
them (temporarily), he shall be free from
tax. Further, just as the city governor
adjudicates between the citizens, so the
head synagogue officer is to decide every
case that may arise between Jews or
against them. But if, by chance, he can
not decide, the case shall be brought
before the bishop and his chamberlains.
Night watches, guards, fortifications, they
shall provide only for their own district,
the guards, indeed, in common with the
servants. Nurses and servants they shall
be permitted to have from among us.
Slaughtered meat which, according to their
law, they are not permitted to eat, they
can sell to Christians, and Christians may
buy it. Finally, as the crowning mark of
kindness, I have given them laws better
than the Jewish people has in any city of
the German empire.

Lest any of my successors diminish this favor and privilege, or force them to pay greater tribute, on the plea that they acquired their favorable status unjustly, and did not receive it from a bishop, I have left this document as a testimony of the above mentioned favors. And that the remembrance of this matter may last through the centuries, I have corroborated it under my hand and seal, as may be seen below.

Given on the fifteenth of September, in the year of the Incarnation 1084, in the twelfth year since the above mentioned bishop commenced to rule in this state."

This document mentions one peculiarity of legislation in regard to the Jews, to which a few words may be devoted. The bishop states that one of the great favors granted the Jews of his diocese was that a Jew passing through the city could lodge with the Jews during his temporary stay without having to pay a tax for the privilege. In the light of known facts, this was, indeed, a noteworthy concession. In most German cities a non-resident Jew was not permitted to stay, even over night ; to stop for a longer time was altogether out of the question. Other cities granted the privilege, but only for a fixed pecuniary consideration. The privileges here granted are remarkable, and the bishop is quite correct in his statement that his Jews lived under more favorable laws than those in any other German city.

The real reason that prompted churchmen to legislate that Jews should occupy separate quarters is given in the following clause taken from the proceedings of the ecclesiastical synod held at Breslau in the year 1266 :

"Since the land of Poland is a new acquisition in the body of Christianity, lest perchance the Christian people be, on this account, the more easily infected with the superstition and depraved morals of the Jews dwelling among them * * * we command that the Jews dwelling in this province of Gnesen shall not live among the Christians, but shall have their houses near or next to one another in some sequestered part of the state or town, so that their dwelling place shall be separated from the common dwelling place of the Christians by a hedge, a wall or a ditch."[56]

The third provincial council of Ravenna, held in 1311, desiring to put an end to the free commingling of Christians and Jews, apparently in vogue in that province, decreed, among other restrictive measures, one in regard to the habitation of the Jews :

"Jews shall not dwell longer than a month anywhere, except in those places in which they have synagogues."[57]

It appears, however, that the commands of this council were not very much respected, for another held in the same place in 1317 deals more stringently with the same subject. The fourteenth rubric of this council begins, "Although the Jews are tolerated by the church, yet they ought not to be tolerated to the detriment or severe injury of the faithful ; because it frequently happens that they return to Christians contumely for favors, contempt for familiarity. Therefore, the provincial council held at Ravenna some time since (*see above*), thinking that many scandals have arisen from their too free commingling with Christians, decreed that they should wear a wheel of yellow cloth on their outer garments, and their women a like wheel on their heads, so that they may be distinguished from Christians," and then it continues, in reference to our subject: "And Jews shall not dwell longer than a month anywhere except in those places in which they have synagogues. But because some, not being able to abstain from forbidden things, disregard the sound decree of the aforementioned council, and pretend ignorance, a penalty shall teach them to know how grave an offense it is to disregard ecclesiastical decrees ; and with the approbation of the sacred council, desiring to prevent this offense hereafter, we warn all clerics as well as laymen of our province, and we decree that two months after the publication of this decree no one shall erect houses for Jews, nor rent or sell them any already built, nor under any pretense grant them (any of their houses), or permit them to occupy them. If any one

acts contrary to this, he shall by that very
deed incur excommunication, from which
he cannot be absolved until he shall satisfy
the above mentioned requirements."[55]

In this manner the Jews were to be
made impossible. Not even a separate
quarter was granted them. No new settlement of Jews was to be permitted anywhere. They had to be satisfied with the
permission to live, in the province of Ravenna, in places in which they chanced to
have a synagogue.

The council of Valencia, in Spain, held
in 1388, went further, and defined clearly
the habitations that Jews might occupy.
Its regulations include Saracens, Jews and
Saracens being placed in the same category as contaminating Christians. By
associating with them, "the faithful incur
serious danger to body and mind," as
it was put. The church dignitaries expressed themselves thus : " We decree, that
Jews and Saracens shall no longer be permitted to have houses, inns or other dwelling places among Christians, nor Christians among Jews and Saracens ; but Jews

and Saracens shall confine themselves to the limits assigned to them in certain cities and places. Where the aforesaid Jews and Saracens have not had limits or confines of this kind assigned to them for habitation, there shall be designated, and assigned to them in the aforementioned cities and places, certain quarters separated from the habitations of the Christians, within which they shall dwell, nor shall they be permitted under any circumstances to tarry without the said limits. * * * As for Christians who shall presume to live within the quarters assigned, or to be assigned, to Jews or Saracens, if, within two months from the day of publication of these orders in the Cathedral church of the state or diocese in which they dwell, they do not have a care to betake themselves to dwelling among Christians, they shall be forced to this by ecclesiastical censure. If, two months after the limits are set for the Jews and Saracens, or after the said limits have been made by the decree and will of the king, or other ruler, ecclesiastical or temporal, of the state or

place, they are unwilling or neglect to retire
within them, they shall be removed from
Christian communion."[59]

The general church council of Basle,
held in 1434, put the matter very clearly,
when, in its nineteenth session, it decreed,
among other laws affecting the Jews:
"That too great converse with them
(Jews) may be avoided, they shall be compelled to live in certain places in the cities
and towns, separated from the dwelling
place of the Christians and as far from the
churches as possible."[60]

The council of Milan, convened in 1565,
during the papacy of Pius IV, the successor of Paul IV, who had, by special decree,
instituted the Ghetto of Rome, demands in
strong terms the establishment of Ghettos
everywhere. The commands of preceding
councils in this matter had not always met
with obedience, but the example set by
the pope himself in forcing the Jews of
his domain into the terrible Jew quarter
was emulated everywhere.

The words of the Milan council on this
subject are as follows: "We strenuously

demand of the rulers that they shall designate in the different cities a certain place
in which Jews shall live apart from Christians. And if Jews have houses of their
own in (other portions of) the city, they
(the rulers) shall command them to be
sold to Christians within six months, in
actuality and not by any pretended con-
tract."[61]

The decrees given require no commentary. They express explicitly enough the
reasons why the Jews were relegated to
separate quarters. They show also the
development of the sentiments towards
this people. It is a long way from the
mild document of Rüdiger, of Speyer,
which granted them a special district as a
protection, to the harsh and positive commands of the councils.

CHAPTER IV.

THE JUDENGASSE OF FRANKFORT-ON-THE-MAIN.

The best known and most celebrated of all the Ghettos of Germany is that of Frankfort-on-the-Main. Its history is remarkable ; some of the most stirring events in German-Jewish history took place there.

The Jews settled in Frankfort later than in most of the German cities. As late as 1152 no Jews lived there. A congregation was formed only towards the close of the twelfth century. The first authentic notice of the presence of Jews in the city is an account in an old chronicle of a fight between Christians and Jews.

The Jews of Frankfort stood under the direct protection of the emperor up to 1349, the year in which the city bought the right over them, *i. e.*, the right to tax them whenever need and occasion required. It was in this year, after this acquisition

(46)

by the city, that the greatest calamities
befell the Jews, not only in Frankfort, but
throughout Germany. The scourge known
as the Black Death raged throughout Europe. Its victims ran up to thousands and
hundreds of thousands. It is said that the
Jews escaped its ravages, or at least did
not succumb in such great numbers as the
Christian population. The cry was raised
that Jews had poisoned the wells. Then
began one of the most terrible persecutions on record. The reports against
the Jews were spread from place to place
by the Flagellants, those bigoted fanatics
who swept the country like a whirlwind,
everywhere raising the cry of the guilt of
the Jews, and inciting the populace to rob
and exterminate the hated people. Their
residences were burnt to the ground. The
flames that destroyed the Jewish quarter
spread, and a large portion of Frankfort
lay in ashes. The whole Jewish community perished ; at least there is no notice
preserved of any Jews that were saved.
The ground which they had owned fell to
the city. In 1360 permission was again

given to Jews to settle in the city. Money
was needed, and taxable property, all that
Jews were considered to be, was in demand. Their condition after the return
was bearable. They were, as a matter
of course, not in possession of political
rights, nor could they hold office. They
were not taxed according to individual fortune, but had to pay a certain yearly sum
for every Jew, determined upon before-
hand. No Jews could be members of the
Rath, the council of citizens that governed
the affairs of the city. They were not
admitted into any military organization.
At this time, in the fourteenth century,
they could own real estate, and fix their
residence in any portion of the city. They
were not yet compelled to dwell in a certain street, although there was a so-called
Jewish quarter, in which most of the Jews
lived together from choice, for here was
the synagogue. Christians also lived in
that quarter, and between 1364 and 1375
the mayor dwelt there.

The council passed upon the rights of the
Jews in so-called *Judenordnungen*. From

the beginning of the fifteenth century
such an act was passed every three years.
This was a very profitable source of revenue, for the Jews could not gain right of
residence for longer than this period, and
so, every three years, they had to pay
liberally to have the privilege renewed. It
was the sword of Damocles continually
hanging over their heads. The failure to
have a favorable act passed, of course,
meant expulsion, but money was all the
legislators wanted, and by means of money
the Jews succeeded in renewing the trien-
nial lease whenever the time expired.

In the act (*Judenordnung*) of 1460, all
the Jews were commanded to leave the
homes hitherto occupied by them, and
dwell together in one street set aside for
them. This is the decree establishing the
Judengasse or Ghetto. The decree gives
as the reason for instituting the Ghetto
the fact that many Jews lived in the
neighborhood of the chief church of the
city, and this proximity was looked upon
as a contamination and a desecration.
It was nothing short of an affront to

4

the Christian religion for Jews to hold
their services so near a church, since the
noise that the Jews made in chanting
during their devotions disturbed the
Christian service. Furthermore, it was
shameful that Jews should view the holy
host, and hear the church songs, as owing
to the nearness of their dwellings to the
church they could, and, therefore, the
Jews and their synagogue not only had to
be removed from such dangerous proximity to the holy building of the Christians, but, what was more, they had to be
relegated to some portion of the city, and
be shut off by themselves, so that all intercourse between them and the Christians
might be impossible. There was to be no
unduly close intimacy, lest the baneful
influence of the Jews result in harm to the
Christians with whom they might come
into contact.

As early as 1442, the council had been
ordered by Emperor Frederick III to
pass this decree, but it had refused to
obey his mandate. In 1458, the order
was repeated, and the council did his

bidding. The quarter of the city to be
inhabited by the Jews was designated.
In 1460, work was begun on the new
Judengasse, and in 1462 the Jews were
compelled to occupy it. It lay in a sparsely
inhabited portion of the city, and was
separated from the nearest dwellings of
the Christians in such a manner that the
Jews dwelt in a completely secluded portion. It lay on the border between the
old and the new city, on a part of the
dried-up city-moat which ran along the
wall of the old city. By this wall it was
separated from the old city; by another
wall, recently erected, from the new city.
It had three entrances, one at the beginning of the street, another at the end, and
the third in the middle of the wall. The
first two connected it with the new city,
the third with the old.

It must not for a moment be imagined
that the Jews accepted this decree with
equanimity. Up to this time they had
lived on a friendly footing with their
neighbors, and now to be shut up like
marked creatures in a pen, locked every

night, filled them with dismay. They tried
by every means to ward off the crushing
blow. Why, why should they be forced
to leave the dwellings they had hitherto
occupied? They had been law-abiding,
harmless. They addressed a petition to
the council, in which, with the eagerness
of despair, they begged that the decree be
revoked, urging reasons, the strongest they
could find, why this dreaded order should
not be carried into effect. In their petition they said that the street appointed
for their dwelling would be so completely
separated from the city by the city wall
that if they needed help, the city would
not be able to assist them, and on the
other side lived only gardeners and people
employed in the woods by the day. Of
late, too, the Jews had been mocked, and
stoned, and threatened with violence in
the streets into which the gates of the
Ghetto led; how much more would this
be the case if in the future they were compelled to go through those very streets
whenever they went outside of their
"street." Besides, in so isolated a region,

they would be exposed, at the time of the two *messen* or fairs, to the abuse and robbery of the many strangers who came to the city on those occasions. At the close of the petition, they offered, in order to invalidate the chief reason urged for their removal from their present homes, to have the gate opposite the church closed, to content themselves in the future with the one exit on the further side, to build a high wall about their present dwellings, and back of them a second, to sell all the houses standing in the vicinity of the church, and rent houses on the further side, and even to be satisfied to have the entrance to the street on that side put under lock and key.

All this they offered in order that they might maintain their self-respect and prevent the carrying out of the terrible measure which was to make of them, in a more aggravated sense than hitherto, a people apart. In spite of petition and appeal they did not succeed. All the offers they made did not assist their cause. Away from the association with their fellow-men

to the narrow, closed-up "street;" away
from the enjoyment of God's light and air
to the sunless, close atmosphere of the
Gasse; away from house and home to the
prison-like tenements in which for well-
nigh four centuries mind and body were
to be stunted! The unfortunates had a
premonition, as it were, of the terrible effects of this latest outrage perpetrated by
Christian legislation. In 1462 they were
compelled to remove from their dwellings
into the new street selected for them; it
was termed at once New Egypt, because
the enforced settling of the Jews there
showed them to be slaves of the Christians, even as their fathers had been of the
Egyptians. Truly an apt comparison, for
the institution of the Ghetto marked the
beginning of a new slavery, and demon-
strated once again to the devoted people
how powerless they were, and how completely at the mercy of their masters.
They were made to feel that contact with
them was an abomination. Wherever they
gazed the word "excluded" met their
eyes—excluded from civic privileges, ex-

cluded from political office and honor, excluded from the trades, excluded from the army, and now excluded from free contact and conversation with others, as though their touch was unholy, and their proximity a curse.

The houses in the *Gasse* had been erected by the city, also the synagogue, the bath-house, the dance-hall and the Jewish inn. On the other hand, all the houses in which Jews had dwelt became the property of the city, without compensation to the owners, other than the use of those assigned to them in their new street. These houses were by no means given to them as their property; for the privilege of inhabiting them they had to pay an annual sum into the city treasury. One hundred and fifty years later the houses of the Judengasse were at last declared to be the property of their tenants, but not the ground whereon they stood, and in place of the house-rent, which they had had to pay formerly, they now had to pay ground-rent. After 1465 all new buildings in the *Gasse* had to be erected at the expense of the Jews.

It was a most gloomy street, twelve feet broad, in its widest portion fifteen or sixteen feet. A wagon could not turn in it, and, that the great confusion incident upon the many stoppages thus caused might be avoided, the city council had the middle entrance widened. The *Gasse* contained one hundred and ninety houses, built very close together, some of them very high and containing many souls, the one hundred and ninety houses harboring four hundred and forty-five families. In each house there were two or three families, and as the community consisted of between twenty-five hundred and four thousand persons, each house contained, on an average, between thirteen and twenty persons. On account of the extreme narrowness of the street and the height of the buildings on either side, the tops of the buildings seemed almost to touch each other. The sun had little opportunity to penetrate here, and in this confinement the people were compelled to spend their lives. They were forced not only to live here; they could not leave

their "street" even for recreation. The
rest of the city was closed to them. Every
night they were locked in. The gates at
the entrances of the *Gasse* were bolted at
sundown, and not opened till morning,
and on Sundays and all Christian and Jewish holidays they were kept bolted all day.
Only in the most urgent cases was any one
permitted to go outside of the "street,"
and then only by a small door, built in each
gate. It might seem that all means of ex-
cluding and degrading these people had
been exhausted by shutting them up. But
no! the inventiveness of the legislators
went further. At no time were the Jews
to breathe the same fresh air with the citizens of the city. In spite of their dark,
close, unhealthy dwelling place, they could
not go forth in leisure hours to walk on
the public promenades. By special legislation it was enacted that no Jew should
walk in the *Stadt Allee*, the public pleas-
ance, the only place in the city, at that
time, for promenading. When, somewhat
later, the moats and ramparts surrounding the city were converted into squares

planted with trees and flowers, the Jews were not permitted to use them, but had to confine themselves to the path leading to them. Can ingenuity go further in fastening the marks of disgrace on an unfortunate community? They were forbidden not only to live in the locality which they might prefer, but to enjoy the invigorating air of God, a right denied not even to the beasts of the field.

There were, too, some streets of the city, to say nothing of the public squares, that they scarcely dared tread upon. So, for example, they were absolutely forbidden to walk across the *Pfarreisen*, that is, the spot adjoining the chief church, or through the thoroughfares (employed as passages) leading to other churches, or over the so-called *Holz und Zimmergraben*. If a Jew presumed to walk on any of these forbidden places, his hat was snatched from his head by passers-by. The *Roemerberg*, the space in front of the *Roemer* or *Rathhaus*, they could use only at the time of the fairs (*messen*), and then only on the east side, the side opposite the city hall.

Yes, there was one occasion on which the contamination of the Jew's presence was suffered even on the side of the space on which the city hall stood. That was when the Jews, on New Year's Day, entered the city hall with their gift of fine spices, which they were expected to give to every councilman, to express their allegiance to the city fathers, and to convey their gratitude for the precious privilege of being cramped in a dark, gloomy, unhealthy spot. This was the only occasion on which a Jew could enter the hall from the front; if, at any other time, he had business that required his presence in the city hall, he had to enter from the rear.

Not only were there certain districts of the city in which Jews were forbidden to appear, but even on the streets on which it was understood that they might walk, they were not free from the abuse and insults of the populace. The cry of *hep! hep!* resounded whenever the unfortunates showed themselves. They were chased through the streets; stones and mud were flung at them, and they dared not retaliate. Three years after their transfer to the *Gasse*, the city council issued a special law forbidding any one to strike Jews, or assail them with insulting epithets on the streets. Such laws, however, were of little avail. The Jews were considered public property as far as the right to revile, abuse, and torment was concerned. Every street urchin looked upon the Jew as a subject for ridicule, and the most venerable, the wisest and the most learned Jew was compelled to take off his hat before any Christian *gamin* who called out "*Jud', mach mores! Jud', mach mores!*" That in spite of all these abuses and hardships Jews remained in Frankfort proves that they were subjected to the same treatment in other places, and were willing to submit to outrages upon honor for the mere permission to live in any quarter, however uninviting. They had to be thankful for this privilege, and were happy if the insults and abuses were not aggravated into robbery, pillage and murder.

The *Judengasse* of Frankfort mirrors in

its story and in the vicissitudes of the lives
of its inhabitants the sad, heartrending and
tragic history of the Jews of Europe in
the centuries during which it existed. The
waves of persecution passed over it, the
fires of oppression played about it, the
stones of religious hatred battered it, but
still the Jew lived on, toiled on, suffered
on. The two most calamitous affairs in
the *Gasse* were the Pfefferkorn and Fettmilch incidents, and because they are
typical of like incidents elsewhere, and
left a deep impress on the community, a
short account of them will not be out of
place in the history of the *Judengasse* of
Frankfort.

John Pfefferkorn was a converted Jew.
He had been a butcher and, as common
report had it, had been discovered in the
act of stealing. After his conversion to
Christianity, like so many of the same ilk,
he proceeded to vilify his former co-religionists in order to give evidence of zeal
for his new religion. It is supposed that
he was the tool of the Dominicans of
Cologne, whose palms itched for Jewish

wealth, chief among them being Jacob van
Hoogstraten, the grand inquisitor. Beginning with the year 1507, Pfefferkorn issued
a number of writings against the Jews. In
that year appeared his *Judenspiegel*, in
which he heaps accusations upon the Jews,
and shows what is necessary to convert
them to Christianity. One of the means
he mentions points to his later course of
action. He says that all the books of the
Jews, the Talmud, prayer-books, all except
the Bible, should be taken from them and
destroyed, for they are the source of their
obstinacy, being directed against Christianity. The next year witnessed the publication of his diatribe, "The Confessions
of the Jews," and in 1509 appeared his
pamphlet, "The Enemy of the Jews," in
which he again made an attack on Jewish
books. These publications against the
Jews were undoubtedly intended to pre-
pare the public mind for active steps
against them. Through the recommenda-
tion of Cunigunda, abbess of a convent in
Munich, Pfefferkorn obtained an interview
with her brother, Emperor Maximilian,

whom he induced to issue an order com-
manding the Jews to deliver to him (Pfefferkorn) all books containing anything against
Christianity, against the Pentateuch, or
the Prophets. He was to be sole judge,
and his authority was to extend throughout the empire. On his return from Padua,
before which the emperor was encamped,
Pfefferkorn stopped at Stuttgart to see the
celebrated scholar, John Reuchlin, whom
he hoped to induce to help him in execut-
ing the order. In this, however, he did not
succeed, as the great humanist, although
he expressed approval of the suppression
of books that vilified the Christian religion,
excused himself from engaging in the
work. Pfefferkorn, baffled in his purpose
of obtaining the assistance and counte-
nance of Germany's greatest scholar, proceeded alone on his journey, and began
operations at Frankfort. On Friday, the
28th of September, the eve of the Feast
of Tabernacles, he appeared in the synagogue with three priests and two town-
councilors. In spite of the protests of the
Jews, he seized all the books he could lay

hold of. The next day he was to search
the private houses, but the Jews objected
so vehemently against the desecration of
the Sabbath that it was put off till Monday.
They saw and felt the danger coming.
They knew that this confiscation of books
was only an introduction to the assaults
on property and life bound to follow, although, at the time, they did not know
that Pfefferkorn was hand in glove with
the Dominicans, nor of the designs of the
latter upon the wealth of the Jews. Excited by the confiscation, and divining what
might follow, they put forth every effort
to have Pfefferkorn's proceedings checked.
With the aid of the archbishop, whose dignity had been affronted, because he had
not been consulted, they succeeded in obtaining a stay of the proceedings. Nothing
daunted, Pfefferkorn again visited the emperor, and succeeded in obtaining a second
order, more explicit than the first. It
named the committee of inquiry to look
into the Jewish books, and among its members were Hoogstraten, the grand inquisitor of the Dominican order ; John Reuch-

lin, and Victor von Carben, "formerly a
rabbi and now a priest." To the great
surprise of the conspirators, Reuchlin declined to serve, and wrote a defense of all
Jewish books except such as contained direct aspersions on Christianity. In it, he
told, in rather plain words, his opinion of
Pfefferkorn. The Jews were saved, as the
fight was now on between Reuchlin and
the Pfefferkorn party, that is, the Dominicans. Publications containing most bitter
recriminations appeared on both sides.
The friends of the two parties took up
the cudgels, too, and the result was that
Pfefferkorn was so belabored that he exposed himself to the ridicule of all times.
The greatest satire of the Middle Ages, the
Epistolæ Obscurorum Virorum appeared
anonymously at this time. These letters
are supposed to be the production of
Crotus Rubianus and Ulrich von Hutten.
The Dominicans, who were supposed to
have inspired the actions of Pfefferkorn to
advance their ulterior designs against the
Jews, are ridiculed in the sharpest possible
manner. Pfefferkorn, too, comes in for

5

his share of satirical notice, ridicule and abuse. So, for once, the enemy of the Jews was baffled. What had promised to be the beginning of persistent outrages upon the Jews—for the confiscation of their books would have led to serious evils and outbreaks—was nipped in the bud by the fortunate refusal of Reuchlin to have anything to do with the work inaugurated by Pfefferkorn. The Jews emerged from what was unquestionably a great difficulty with the loss of nothing more than what money may have been required to bribe the archbishop and the town councilors to stay the proceedings in the first instance. That they were frightened, we can readily believe. The immediate steps they took saved them.

The other incident to which reference was made above was much more serious in its consequences. The guilds in Frankfort were always very strong. They had a particular animosity against the Jews, and were continually laboring to effect their expulsion from the city. Not succeeding in this, an attack on the Jewish quarter was determined upon. The leader was a baker, Vincent Fettmilch. On August 22, 1614, the attack was made. The Jews, having been warned, did not quietly wait for the attack, but made preparations to resist. They procured arms, removed their wives and children to the cemetery for refuge, locked the gates that led into their street, and barricaded the gate upon which the attack was expected. They then proceeded to the synagogue, and prayed and fasted. While assembled there, they heard the blows upon the gates and the angry cries of the mob. In terror they poured out of the synagogue, men and youths taking up arms to defend themselves. The mob, foiled by the barricade of the gate, broke into the street through a house which stood next to the gate. A bitter fight of eight hours followed; two Jews and one Christian were killed, and many wounded. The Jews, few in number, were gradually overcome. Then began a fearful scene of plunder and destruction. The mob rushed into the houses. They had proceeded about half way through the street

when a band of armed citizens appeared
and drove them out. The Jews, thoroughly frightened, hastened to seek refuge in their cemetery, situated at the end
of the *Gasse*, in which they had placed their
wives and children. They were advised
by the town council to leave the city, since
it could not protect them. On the next
day, they did this, and for one year and a
half they remained away from the city, and
lived in the neighboring towns. In the
meantime, order had been restored, and
steps were taken looking to the return of
the Jews. The leaders of the mob, Fettmilch and six others, were beheaded. On
the very day that this took place, February
28, 1616, the Jews returned. Their return
was celebrated with music. When they
arrived in front of the *Gasse*, they were
formed into a circle, and the new *Judenordnung*, drawn up by the imperial com-
missioners, was read to them. The town
council having shown itself so powerless
to guard them, the protection of the Jews
reverted to the emperor; they once again
became his private property. After their

return into their "street," a large shield
was placed upon each of the three gates,
upon which was painted the imperial eagle
with the inscription, "Under the protection of the Roman Imperial Majesty and
of the Holy Empire." Strange to say, the
Christian population was compelled by
imperial mandate to pay the Jews 175,919
florins indemnity for the loss they had
sustained. In memory of these events, the
Jewish congregation of Frankfort annually
celebrated two events, the 19th of Adar,
as a fast day commemorative of their departure from the city, and the 20th as a
holiday, called Purim Fettmilch, in memory
of their return.

The next event of great importance was
the complete destruction of the *Gasse* by
fire in 1711. The population had greatly
increased, but the space for habitation was
not enlarged. The number of houses did
not increase, and the one hundred and
ninety houses that, in a former day, had
sheltered but two thousand persons, were
now the homes of some eight thousand, according to the smallest calculation the Jew-

ish population at this time. Each house, therefore, on an average harbored forty-one persons. The *Gasse* is an example of the worst evils of the tenement system. On January 14, 1711, fire broke out in the house of the chief rabbi, which stood in the middle of the "street." The cause of the fire was never discovered. It wiped out the Jewish quarter completely, and was called the great Jewish conflagration, in contradistinction to the great Christian conflagration eight years later. The Christian population, as soon as the fact of the raging of the fire became known, hurried to the *Gasse* to give assistance. But the Jews, in an agony of terror, and remembering former days, had locked the gates for fear of plunder, and kept them closed for an hour. When, at last, they opened them the flames had gained great headway. The fire spread throughout the quarter, and with the exception of three houses standing at the extreme end of the street, everything was destroyed. The Jews, now homeless, had to look about for shelter. Some were harbored in Christian

houses. After the "street" was rebuilt,
they lingered in these houses with the
hope that they might be permitted to remain outside the *Gasse*, and have freedom
of residence, but they were all ordered
back in 1716. Some who could not find
shelter in the city, settled in neighboring
towns, until their homes were rebuilt,
while the very poor were placed, by the
town council, in a hospital, to sojourn
there until their dwelling places were restored. The rebuilding began almost at
once. The synagogue was completed by
the autumn of the same year. It stood
until 1854, when the large and beautiful
building, dedicated in 1860, was built in its
place. By the year 1717 all the houses
were rebuilt. In the process of recon-
struction the street was widened by four
feet, so that it was twenty feet wide.
Houses of not more than three stories
were permitted to be built, but most of
them had gables. Back buildings one
story higher were erected, hence the yards
were very small, but by decree each house
had to be six feet from the wall along the

back of the *Gasse*. On the houses they were compelled to place signs, with peculiar figures and names, so that they were known as the house of the bear, the dragon, of the white, green, red, black shield, etc. The inhabitants were designated according to these figures, e. g. the Jew N. N. *zum Bären*, etc. The Rothschild family received its name from the red shield that marked its house.

The "street" again suffered from fire in 1774 and in 1796. In the former instance twenty-one houses were destroyed. The inhabitants rented houses without the *Gasse* for two years until their homes were rebuilt, when they again had to return. In the latter year, the fire assumed larger dimensions, and one hundred and forty houses were destroyed. This was during the bombardment of the city by the French under Kleber, July 12 to 14. This portion, called *Bornheimer Strasse*, was soon rebuilt, and very greatly improved by being widened and having fine buildings erected upon it.

The *Judengasse* was now approaching

its end. Better days were beginning to
dawn for the Jews. The breath of freedom and emancipation characteristic of the
close of the last and the beginning of this
century was wafted upon them, too. In
1806, Frankfort and some neighboring
districts were placed under the jurisdiction of the enlightened and kindly Karl
Theodor von Dalberg, the *Fürst Primas*.
He took great interest in the improvement of the Jews of his domain, and
assisted them greatly in their efforts
towards self-advancement, in the founding
of schools, and the like. In 1811 he
granted them full rights of citizenship,
but in the reaction that ensued shortly
after, he was deprived of his rule, and the
Jews lost the rights he had granted them.

After the fall of Napoleon and the con-
sequent relapse into mediævalism and mediæval legislation against the Jews in
the German states and cities, the Jews
of Frankfort suffered, too. The *hep-hep*
cry again resounded in the streets, the
Jewish houses were attacked, the Jews
driven from the promenades. In conse-

quence of these disturbances many Jewish
families left the city. The second and
third decades of this century were a gloomy
time for the Jews of Germany ; the emancipation question was uppermost, and gal-
lantly did the Jewish champions, headed
by Gabriel Riesser, conduct the struggle.
In this agitation the Jews of Frankfort
were likewise concerned, and in 1848 they
once again gained the right of citizenship,
but in 1850 they lost it, to receive it a
third time in 1864. Since then they have
retained it, and, of course, as far as political rights are concerned, are now on an
equal footing with all citizens of the German Empire.

A few words more about the *Gasse.*
Even after it had been rebuilt after the
great fire of 1711, it was as gloomy and
cheerless as it had been. The high, gabled
houses built so close together naturally
kept out all sunlight and air. So it continued—except in the western portion,
which was burnt in 1796, and rebuilt, as
stated above—until the year 1830, when a
large number of the houses were con-

demned by the city authorities because of
their ruinous condition, and their removal
from both sides of the street produced
empty spaces through which the air could
circulate. As soon as the note of emancipation was struck, in the beginning of the
century, many Jews removed from the
Gasse, nor were they compelled to return
thither. The empty houses were rented,
and occupied by the poorer classes of
Christians, so that, except in name and
memory, it was no longer distinctively the
Judengasse, the Jewish quarter. Two of
the houses were of especial interest, that
in which Löb Baruch, or, as he is known
in German literature, Ludwig Börne, was
born, and the ancestral home of the Rothschild family.

About ten years ago, the houses in the
old portion of the street fell in because of
age and decay. They were demolished and
removed, with the exception of the Rothschild house. This portion of the street
was then broadened to a width equal to
that of *Bornheimer Strasse*, the section of
the old street which had been improved

and widened in the early part of the century, and the two portions became one street, the present *Börne Strasse*, a wide thoroughfare, possessing no similarity to the old, narrow *Gasse*. A great portion of the street remains to be built up. The old wall that separated the street in the early days from the old quarter of the city is still standing; a street leading to *Börne Strasse* has been broken through it.

One important relic of the old time is still preserved; at the very end of what is now *Börne Strasse*, and what was formerly the *Judengasse*, enclosed by a high wall, and hidden from the view of the passer-by, lies the old cemetery[62] of the Frankfort Jewish congregation, containing, with the exception of some in the cemetery at Worms, the oldest epitaph in western Europe. This was the spot to which the Jews removed their wives and children and helpless ones during the persecutions and the attacks made on the *Gasse* by the mobs.[63] The cemetery is now in a sad state of neglect; many of the stones have fallen to the ground, and lie in

great confusion, and many are beginning
to crumble. In the eastern end of the
graveyard the graves are thick and close
together. Near the entrance there are
but few tombstones, only a number of
small groups, here and there. This is explained by the surmise that the eastern
portion was set aside for the burial of
Frankfort Jews, while the smaller groups
of graves are those of small communities in the vicinity of Frankfort, which
made use of this burying ground for the
interment of their dead. The cemetery
is large, and contains over six thousand
tombstones. The inscriptions on these
stones offer much material to the student
of Jewish history and customs. "Of the
immense store which the cemetery at
Frankfort-on-the-Main offers, only a slight
portion has been published."[64] This statement is true, but all the inscriptions have
been copied through the instrumentality
of Dr. Horowitz, the rabbi of the new
synagogue overlooking the old cemetery.
He has collated them, and ere long the
learned world may be enriched by their

publication. The earliest tombstone in
the cemetery dates from the year 1272;
the last burial took place in 1828, when
the town council decreed that it should
be no longer used for purposes of burial,
and that it should lie undisturbed for one
hundred years. The graves are two and
three deep, perhaps more, the surface
having been covered over with additional
layers of earth whenever the available space
had been used. This appears from two
facts : in the first place, the burial ground
proper is higher than the adjacent walks ;
and there are often two or three stones
on the same grave. The stones are of red
sandstone, with the exception of the oldest,
which are gray. These have stood the
wear of time best ; they are still thoroughly
well preserved, while many of the later
ones are crumbling. The inscriptions are
for the most part legible, and some of the
stones display very artistic work, the sign
of the house in which the departed had
lived often being carved on them,[65] so that
there are stones ornamented with figures
of dragons, bears, lions, stars, and the like.

The most beautiful piece of work is on a stone belonging to a family Trach (*drache*) —a dragon most artistically hewn, and sculptured flowers on the rim.

Very celebrated rabbis lie buried here, in fact, all the rabbis of the Frankfort congregation, among them the author of the celebrated *P'ne Yehoshuah* and Rabbi Pinchas Hurwitz.[66]

Walking through this cemetery, where now all is peace and rest and quiet, I could not but think of the terrible days of the past, and the scenes this spot had witnessed, and there arose before me the vision of the hundreds of unfortunates, who, in that terrible night of September 1, 1614, during the Fettmilch attack, were massed in the " home of the dead," about the graves of their fathers. When all opposition was seen to be fruitless, the men repaired to the place to which, in the earlier period of the affray, they had moved their wives and children. All hope seemed cut off. "We will sanctify the name of God," cried they. They donned their shrouds, and determined to meet death

rather than disgrace. They prepared themselves for the supreme moment by giving
voice to the confession of their sinfulness
and their belief in the divine justice. With
terror and trembling they awaited the
dawning of another day. A report came
to their ears that the mob had disagreed.
Yes, it was true ; by the aid of the town
council they made their escape from the
cemetery, and with their bare lives, homeless, houseless, they left Frankfort to seek
shelter in the surrounding towns.[67]

A troubled vision of the night of the
past, by contrast making the present all
the brighter!

To return now to the Ghetto : The
houses of the *Gasse* were all very much
alike. They were frame, with the exception of one stone house. On account of
the gloom of the street they were very
dark inside. Some points of their inner
construction furnish eloquent testimony of
the times in which they were built and the
continual fear of attack and persecution in
which their occupants lived. Many of the
houses had no steps leading to the roof,

only a ladder, which could be pulled up
by those who had fled to the roof from
their pursuers. For a like reason, namely,
protection in time of danger from the outbreaks of mobs, the cellars of neighboring
houses were connected by doors, concealed
by cupboards. Through these doors the
occupants of the houses, if hard pressed,
could flee into the cellar of the adjoining
residence. Thank God that such precau-
tions are no longer necessary! In the new
and better time, the Jew is not marked off
by his place of residence; justice being
done, the marks of oppression have disappeared. The *Judengasse* of Frankfort is
no more. The memories of the days of
persecution are permitted to sink into ob-
livion. The veil of forgiveness has been
dropped over them by those so deeply
wronged, and in this new time the Jews of
Frankfort have assimilated themselves
with their fellow citizens, and stand on an
equal footing with them in all civic interests.

6

CHAPTER V.

THE JUDENSTADT OF PRAGUE.

To the tourist visiting the city of Prague, by far the most interesting spot in this gloomy, gray place is the old Jewish quarter lying on the right bank of the river Moldau, of old designated *Judenstadt*, but now known as *Josefstadt*. This ancient quarter with its narrow streets, its old synagogues, its burying ground famed in story, its town hall reminiscent of the days when the Jewish administrative body exercised judicial functions, its legends, its history, cannot but awaken a mournful train of thought in him who, permitting his mind to dwell on the past, recalls the sad, sad fate of this Ghetto, with one exception probably the oldest Jewish settlement north of the Alps. Not a single street, as in Frankfort, but a whole section of the city did the Jewish quarter of Prague comprise. It is standing much as it was,

but it is no longer the compulsory dwelling
place of Jews, although largely inhabited
by them. Many Christians, especially
of the poorer classes, now dwell there too.
The walls and gates, which in the old days
separated the Jewish quarter from the remainder of the city, have disappeared, but
the spot in which they stood is still pointed
out. The streets scarcely deserve to be
called such, so narrow, crowded, dark and
gloomy are they. The houses on either
side tower aloft, shutting out the sunlight,
so that even on a bright day the lanes rest
in shadow. Many stirring scenes have
these streets witnessed. Had the stones
tongues, what stories could they tell of
mobs and plunder, of persecution and
murder, of incendiarism and robbery, of
fight and strife, of bravery and martyr-
dom, of silent suffering and heroic endurance! The history of the Jewish community of Prague dates from days long past,
through many centuries, during which it
proudly claimed to be the greatest and
most important congregation in Europe.
Great names of celebrated rabbis, writers

and heroes, shed lustre over that old
Judenstadt, and make it shine with a glory
that will never fade. Dark spots there
are, too, of superstition, for there is no
Jewish community in the world so full of
superstitions, legends and traditions as
this of Prague, but these gradually disappear in the light of investigation, while the
true and great things there thought and
accomplished live on forever.

The early history of the Jews of Prague
is shrouded in mystery. Concerning the
time when they first settled in the city, or
entered Bohemia, there is no authentic information. The statement that a flourish-
ing Jewish community existed in Prague
during the time of the second Temple
must be regarded as purely legendary.
That there were many Jews in Prague
during the earliest Christian centuries may
be true, but there is no contemporary evidence of the fact; that Jews may have
lived in the city in quite ancient times is
very possible, but the date of their first
entrance into the land and their earliest
settlement cannot be fixed. There can be

no doubt that Jews lived in Bohemia and
in Prague in heathen times, before the
introduction of Christianity in the tenth
century.[68] Their first settlement lay on
the left bank of the river Moldau. When
their numbers increased and their quarters
became too small, they were assigned, in
all likelihood in the eleventh century, a
new and larger dwelling place on the right
bank of the river, the present *Josefstadt.*
The Jews were not compelled to live in
this one section. They dwelt in various
quarters of the city until the middle of
the fifteenth century (1473), when, after
a destructive pestilence that decimated the
population, all the Jews not yet in the
Judenstadt determined to cast in their lot
with their brethren there, and so all were
merged into the one great community,[69]
which became "a mother in Israel," an
influential congregation. Great rabbis
flourished there, schools of Jewish learning arose and prospered, men and women
whose names are honored in history lived
their life in this Ghetto, and all the phe-
nomena that characterize mediæval Jewish

history appeared there. Sacred memories,
indeed, this Ghetto cherishes, and dark
happenings, too, that speak ill for human
kind; grand achievements of learning,
heroism and philanthropy brighten its an-
nals, but pages blackened with the record of
internal strife and superstition peep forth,
too. In this long history of centuries are
mirrored the manifold acts that make up
the sum of human endeavor, and the record
of the Jewish community of Prague, with
its lights and shadows, its glories and de-
gradations, presents a faithful picture of
the course of human life as it ebbed and
flowed in the narrow confines of Jewry
during the centuries that preceded the
emancipation of the present.

First, as to the external history of the
community. It was subject to many persecutions and expulsions and extortions.
The story is much the same as that of the
Jews everywhere. During the crusades,
the time fraught with so much misery for
these hapless ones, when the mobs fell
upon the Jewish communities, and murder,
carnage and plunder held high carnival,

the *Judenstadt* of Prague came in for its
share of the gentle mercies of the crusaders. Drunk with the blood of the victims
whom they had slaughtered or driven to
death in the German cities, the crusaders
came to Bohemia, attacked the Jews
of Prague, dragged them to baptism,
and killed those who resisted. In vain
good Bishop Cosmas preached against
these terrible proceedings; the crusaders
paid no heed to his words.[70] This was in
the year 1099. During the third crusade
the mobs on their way to Palestine passed
through Bohemia, and in Prague demanded
money from the Jews. They refused to
comply with this request, and the crusaders resorted to violence. It is refreshing
to note that the Jews resisted so successfully that the crusaders were forced to draw
off without having accomplished their object.[71]

In the year 1389 occurred the most terrible persecution to which the Jews of
Prague were ever subjected. On Easter
Sunday (April 18) of that year, a priest
carrying the pyx was passing through the

Jewish quarter. Some Jewish children were playing in the sand on the street (it was the last day of Passover), pelting one another with pebbles. Some of the pebbles chanced to strike the priest, which so enraged him and those who accompanied him that they abused the children shamefully. The parents of the children, alarmed by their cries, hastened to the spot to aid them. The priest now hurried away into the city, crying aloud that his office had been desecrated by the Jews, that they had pelted him with stones, so that the host had fallen from his hands. Thereupon the citizens of Prague descended upon the homes of the Jews, and offered them the alternative of baptism or death. The Jews, refusing to forswear their faith, were murdered by the thousands on that day and the following night. Many Jews, among others the aged rabbi, killed their own dear ones to save them from the fury of the mob, and then themselves. The synagogues, with one exception, were destroyed, and even the dead were not left in peace. The great cemetery was devastated, the tombstones were destroyed[72] (so that there is now no stone in the cemetery dating from earlier than the fifteenth century), and the corpses were disinterred, stripped, and left to rot on the streets. The pope, more merciful, issued a bull on July 2, denouncing these barbarities, and referring to the edict of Innocent IV, which forbade the forcible baptism of the Jews, or the interference with them on their holidays. The king, Wenceslaus, declared that the Jews deserved their fate, because they had had the hardihood to leave their houses on Easter Sunday and appear on the streets. It was a canon law that the Jews should not be seen on the streets during Holy Week, and the law was wise, for collisions were bound to take place between the followers of the two religions. Some Jews, without doubt, would take occasion to mock, so that the command to remain in-doors was well-intentioned. Indeed it has been maintained that this terrible persecution arose from the fact that some Jews mocked the priest.[73]

Many of the greatest evils were brought
upon the Jews by apostates, who often
thought to ingratiate themselves with their
new comrades by bringing accusations and
spreading calumnies against their old co-
religionists. Their method usually was to
declare that here and there in the Jewish
writings there was some attack upon Christianity or its founder. By specious argu-
ments they worked up the easily influenced
populace and priesthood (for the most part
ignorant and not understanding one word
of Hebrew) against the Jews, and in spite
of protest, declarations that the accusations were false, the deposition of clear
proof, and the explanation of the passages
in question, the unfortunates, condemned
by public opinion no matter what they
might say, always had to suffer. As though
their cup of bitterness were not full enough,
the Jews had to bear with ills inflicted on
them by those who had gone forth from
their own midst. At the end of the fourteenth century (1399), one of these converted Jews, by name Pesach, changed
into Peter with his change of religion,

leveled a new accusation against his former
brethren in faith by declaring that a blas-
phemous charge against Jesus is contained
in that sublime concluding prayer of the
Jewish service known as *Alenu*, which gives
expression to the belief in the unity of
God and to the hope for the time when
superstition and idolatry will disappear, and
God alone will be recognized. The lie
was credited, many Jews of Prague were
arrested, seventy-seven executed, and three
publicly burnt.[74]

So rose and fell the waves of Jewish
life ; the Jews were only a tolerated class.
The story is the same all over Europe ;
they were subject to caprice of ruler and
mob. It must not be imagined that there
was continual persecution ; there were
many intervals of peace, in which the regular avocations of life were calmly pursued,
but at any moment the peace might be
broken, and new miseries fall to the lot of
the inhabitants of the Ghetto. Of course,
the petty persecutions to which Jews
were subjected everywhere, the inhabitants
of the Prague Ghetto experienced. The

compulsion to wear the distinguishing
mark on their clothes, the prohibition to
employ Christian nurses for their children,
and many other like prohibitions embittered their lives, but they grew accustomed
to these things, too.   They had to pay extra taxes of various kinds.   Time and again
they were threatened with expulsion from
the land, and it was only by the ex-
penditure of great sums that they succeeded in staying the execution of the decree.   Rulers and people seem to have
lost all human feeling in dealing with the
Jews.   Even in the possession of their
books and writings they were not left
undisturbed.   The confiscations and burn-
ing of Jewish books, alleged to contain
blasphemies against Christianity and its
founder, form an interesting chapter in the
account of the mediæval oppression of the
Jews.[75]   For instance, in the year 1559,
all Jewish books and manuscripts found
in the Jewish quarter of Prague, including
prayer books, eighty hundred-weight in all,
were confiscated, and sent to Vienna.   In
the same year a conflagration broke out

in the Jewish quarter, and destroyed a
great number of dwellings. Instead of
assisting the unfortunates to quench the
fire, the Christian populace threw weak
women into the flames, and plundered
where they could. Two years later, in 1561,
Ferdinand I, who had long been working
towards that end, ordered their expulsion
from the city. For years they had succeeded in preventing the carrying out of
the dread order, but now they were compelled to wander forth. The emperor met
all appeals to reconsider the decree with
the statement that he had vowed to expel
the Jews from Prague, and could not
break his oath. Yet was the expulsion revoked, and that, too, in a most unexpected
and dramatic manner. Mordecai Zemach
Kohen, a Jew of Prague, whose tombstone still stands in the great cemetery, determined, if possible, to rescue his brethren
from the terrible calamity. He journeyed
to Rome, by some means obtained an
audience with Pope Pius IV, received a
dispensation absolving the emperor from
his vow, and the Jews were permitted to
return in March of the following year.[76]

In the beginning of the seventeenth century there were about ten thousand Jews in Prague,[77] and they were quite prosperous. There had been a lull in the persecutions. Under the emperors Rudolph and Matthias the Jewish quarter attained unexampled splendor. Mordecai Meisel, the great benefactor of the Prague Jewish community, lived during this time (1528—1601). The emperors had issued privileges and shown much favor to individual Jews, notably Meisel and Jacob Bassewi. The latter was afterwards ennobled on account of his services to the imperial house, took the name of von Treuenberg, and was permitted to adopt a coat of arms (blue lion and eight red stars on a blue background). These privileges to individual Jews redounded to the benefit of the community at large, and the people enjoyed happy days. But with the Bohemian revolt in 1619, an early incident of the bloody Thirty Years' War, the happy condition of the Jews' quarter changed almost in a twinkling. The adherents of the Protestant elector palatine, Frederick,

king of Bohemia, made the Jewish quarter the object of pillaging attack, because of the loyalty of the Jews to the
Catholic imperial house. This loyalty
brought them fitting reward. At the celebrated battle of White Mountain, November 8, 1620, the imperial troops gained
a decided victory, and at once proceeded
to invest the capital city of Prague. Now
followed days and weeks of plunder and
bloodshed, but, marvelous to say, the
Jews, always the first victims on such occasions, were unexpectedly protected. The
commander of the imperial forces, remembering the faithfulness of the Jews to his
cause, stationed guards before the gates
of the Jewish quarter, and thus this section of the city was saved from the horrors of war rampant in all other quarters
of the town. In remembrance of this unexpected deliverance, the rabbinate appointed the day, the 14th of Marcheshwan,
an annual fast and feast day, the forenoon
to be spent in fasting, in memory of the
tribulation and terror of the people before
deliverance came ; the afternoon in feast-

ing, in memory of the salvation. This day
was known as the Prague Purim.[73] The
rich Jews of Prague were granted permission to purchase the houses abandoned by
the Protestants who had sought safety in
flight.

Emperor Ferdinand continued to show
favor to the Jews of Prague. In 1623 he
issued a *privilegium* from Ratisbon, in
which it was decreed that the Jews of
Prague were not to be held responsible
for the debts of the Jews of the rest of
Bohemia, and that they need pay no higher
taxes than the Christians. The allegations
of the elders of the community of Prague
were to be respected, and the Jews of
Bohemia were to be permitted to pursue
trade without hindrance. In 1628 he
enlarged these privileges, and ordered the
Jews to pay 40,000 fl. yearly, and so free
themselves from all other taxes.

During the whole long struggle, the
Jews continued faithful to the imperial
house. The war was ended in Prague,
where it had begun. When the Swedes
approached the city, and besieged it, the

Jewish quarter, which lay on the bank of
the river, was especially open to their attacks, and the Jews threw up a redoubt,
known as the Jews' redoubt. The quarter
was bombarded, and the inhabitants suffered greatly. When the nobles and other
inhabitants of Prague went forth to do
battle with the enemy, the Jews were left
behind to patrol and guard the city. They
were continually engaged in repairing the
gaps made in the fortifications and in
throwing up new redoubts. Several of
them lost their lives. The treaty of West-
phalia brought the contest to an end, and
the evil days were past. In celebration of
the cessation of the siege and the deliverance of the city, the Jews had a public procession with music, and at the head of the
line of march were carried two flags presented to them by former emperors. As
a reward for their bravery and constancy
during the siege, they were given permission to have a small bell in the Jewish
town hall to call the people together when
important matters were to be decided.[79]
Besides, in recognition of their action on

7

this occasion, Emperor Ferdinand III in
creased their privileges and rights by
granting them permission to live in all
imperial cities and possessions, from which
they were not to be expelled without the
knowledge of the emperor. They were also
permitted to engage in all trades and industries except the manufacture of arms.[80]
But dark days were again coming. In
1679 the Jewish quarter was visited by a
conflagration; eight years later, in 1687, a
second conflagration devastated the quarter, and laid it almost completely in ruins.
The Jews were, therefore, necessitated to
seek shelter in Christian homes. The
archbishop forbade the priests to adminis-
ter the rite of extreme unction to Christians who had received Jews into their
homes. When he refused to reconsider
the heartless order, the people appealed
to the emperor, who had shown himself
more humane. He replied that he knew
it to be forbidden for Jews and Christians
to live together, but that he considered
the present an exceptional case. He
warned the Jews, however, not to mock
or scoff at the Christians.[81]

The last expulsion of the Jews from Prague took place in 1744. On the 23d of December of the preceding year, Empress Maria Theresa had issued a decree that by the end of 1744 all Jews must leave Bohemia. Entreaties, expostulations availed naught. With the exception of a very few favored ones, all the Jews had to leave Prague. The usual consequences of such a measure followed ; trade languished and real estate declined in value, for the sudden withdrawal of a large, active and industrious portion of the population always has a deleterious effect. The petitions for the return of the Jews on the part of the authorities, the tradesmen and the populace of the city generally, became so urgent and persistent that in 1748 the empress found herself compelled to yield, and granted the Jews permission to return, on condition that they paid, in conjunction with their co-religionists in Moravia and Silesia, an annual Jew-tax of 300,000 florins in addition to the regular taxes. This tax was exacted up to the year 1848.[52]

Towards the close of the century, the

new spirit began to affect the reigning house of Hapsburg, too, and Emperor Joseph II commenced to improve the condition of the Jews. The emancipation of the Jews went steadily forward, sustaining reverses at times, it is true, but the freedom making itself felt everywhere could not but affect the condition of the Jews, and in 1848—wondrous year—the Jewish quarter or Ghetto of Prague ceased to be the compulsory dwelling place of the Jews. They were permitted to live in all quarters of the city; gradually the gates and walls were removed; poorer classes of Christians moved into the vacated houses. The quarter with many of its old landmarks, which will be described briefly, still stands, occupied, in great part, by Jews, but there is a vast difference between the voluntary domicile of this day and the compulsory dwelling place of the dark centuries of the past.

A few of the salient events of the outer history of the Jews of Prague having been given, some pages may now be devoted to the inner life, the description of the Ghetto and its prominent features.

The Jewish community of Prague was, with the exception of that of Amsterdam, the largest in Europe during mediæval times. The *Judenstadt* was large, and was separated from the city by nine gates, which were locked and barred every night from within. The Jews had their own jurisdiction, and the directory, composed of the chief men of the community, super-intended the police regulations. Civil suits were decided by the college of rabbis. In short, the Jewish community was to a certain extent self-ruling, and in this differed from other European Jewish communities. From early times this had been the case. In the year 1268, by a friendly decree of Ottokar II, the Jews were released from the jurisdiction of the aldermen of the city, and provision was made for the appoint-ment of a *judex Judæorum*, a judge of the Jews, who was to decide in civil and criminal cases. The synagogue was to be the court of justice, and was declared inviolable. Since decisions were given among the Jews according to the rabbini-cal code, this judge always had to be a

rabbi ; he presided at the sessions of the
court. At the head of the political administration stood the president of the
congregation, known as the *primator*.
As just stated, the synagogue was the
seat of justice. This was the case until
the close of the sixteenth century, when
the town hall, which is still standing, was
built by Mordecai Meisel, and used thereafter for all judicial functions, and the
synagogue was employed for its proper purpose, the holding of religious service. The
town hall is joined to a synagogue known
as the *Hoch-Synagoge*, which served as a
sort of private chapel for the councilors,
and for the fulfilment of religious duties
connected with the dispensation of justice.
The town hall is graced with a tower, on
which is a curious dial with the hours
marked in Hebrew and Arabic numerals.
After the conflagration of 1754, the town
hall was rebuilt (on its door appears the
date 1755), and the bell of the tower re-
cast. On this bell may be read in Hebrew
characters, "renewed in the year 5525,"
i. e. 1764. In 1627, Ferdinand II, the mon-

arch who was so kindly disposed toward
the Jews of the city, declared the *Judenstadt* an independent district, with its own
magistrates and jurisdiction. Two judicial bodies were now formed, a lower and
a higher court. The judges of the lower
court held daily public sessions. They
adjudicated in litigations of small import.
The higher court composed of the college
of rabbis, the chief rabbi at the head, was
the court of appeal, to which cases could
be carried from the lower court, suits of
great importance being brought before it
in the first instance. In 1784 this separate Jewish rabbinical jurisdiction was
abolished. The affairs of the Jewish community were then placed under the supervision of the town magistrate.[83] At present,
since the year 1849, the old town hall
serves as an office building for the direc-
tors of the religious affairs of the congregation.

Directly opposite the town hall stands
an old, venerable structure, not very large,
but the most interesting building in the
whole quarter. The ancient house is

known as the *Alt-neu Synagoge*, the "Old-new synagogue," the building that has stood the wear and tear of time, that has existed through the long, sad history of the ages. Many harrowing scenes of man's inhumanity to man, and many sublime instances of supreme faithfulness and steadfastness even in death have its walls witnessed. Old, centuries old, is the building, and many have been the theories as to the time of its construction. The name, "Old-new synagogue," seems to indicate that at one time the old synagogue was renewed, and in truth, at the first glance it becomes evident that the building consists of two entirely distinct portions, the older, lower story being in the Byzantine style of architecture, the upper, newer in the Gothic. The tradition of the Ghetto has it that the older portion dates from the sixth, the newer from the thirteenth century. Late investigators have concluded that neither is so old ; that the older part was constructed in the twelfth, and the newer in the fourteenth century.[84]

The synagogue is entered by steps leading down to the floor of the building, which lies lower than the street. According to tradition, it was so built in fulfilment of the word of the Psalmist, " Out of the depths have I cried unto Thee, O Lord !" Beautiful and poetical as is this thought, in the light of historical research it has been dissipated, for it has been established that at one time the street was much lower than at present, and that the building was then on a level with the street ; that later the street was raised, and the buiding, now being lower, had to be reached by descending steps. The interior is small and gloomy ; there is no gallery, and the women had to be content with looking through the small windows situated at intervals along the northern wall. A conspicuous object in the synagogue is the great red flag attached to one of the pillars opposite the entrance; ornamented with the shield of David, within it the Swede's hat, and bearing the inscription, " 'The Lord of Hosts, full is the whole earth of His glory'! In the year 5117 A. M.,

(i. e. 1357) his Majesty, Emperor Charles IV, granted the Jews the distinction and the privilege of carrying a flag. This was renewed in the reign of Emperor Ferdinand. Damaged by the wear of time, it is now renewed in honor of our lord, Emperor Charles VI, may God increase his glory! On the occasion of the birth of his exalted son, Archduke Leopold, in the year 1716." The privilege of carrying a flag in their processions was highly prized by the Jews. Whenever an emperor came to Prague, and the Jews formed in procession to meet him, the flag was brought forth. The Swede's hat, embroidered within the shield of David on the flag, is the coat of arms granted the Jews by Ferdinand II, in recognition of their bravery and their services during the siege of the city by the Swedes. The flag is now merely a relic, and has lost its former significance and importance, but the Jews' of Prague still point to it with pride, as the symbol embodying the patriotism of the early inhabitants of the Ghetto and their faithfulness to the government and the land of their residence.

The interior of the synagogue is dark and gloomy. The gloom was until within the past few years much greater even than it is now, the walls being black with the dust and mold of centuries. There was a tradition that these walls had been bespattered with the blood of the martyrs of the great persecution of 1389, and for fear of obliterating the traces, the rabbis continually protested against a cleansing of the walls. This gave the old building a sombre appearance, and increased the natural gloom in which the interior was shrouded, so that it appeared indeed a relic of a sad, dark, gloomy past. Lately the interior has been renovated, and what it may have lost as a relic of sad antiquity, it has gained in cheer. The history of the old house of worship is remarkable. It passed unscathed through fire and flood. In the great conflagrations which visited the Ghetto, and to which allusion has been made, the flames devoured the buildings in its immediate vicinity, but it escaped unharmed, for great efforts were always made to save it. During the devastating inunda-

tions of the river Moldau, to which the
Ghetto, lying on the bank of the stream,
was especially exposed, time and again
buildings were swept away, but the old
synagogue successfully withstood the attacks of water, as it had of fire, and even
during the persecutions, when cruelty ran
riot, and the Ghetto was despoiled by
murderous, plundering mobs, the mad-
dened populace seemed to regard this old
structure with awe, possibly with super-
stitious dread, for never was it despoiled
or ruined. Within its walls, the poor,
hunted creatures gathered in the days of
persecution. At one time, as has been
stated, some met their death there, and
their life-blood stained the walls. Here,
too, they assembled in troubled days to
pray for help and strength. No wonder
that there gathered about it a mass of
legends, superstitions and traditions, that
it became the object of the people's loving
care and solicitude, that it embodied for
them all the glory of their faith, and
became the symbol for the long, sad tale
of their history. Many a larger, more pre-

tentious house of worship has arisen in the
city, but none is and none can ever be regarded with the affection and reverence
that cling to the *Alt-neu Schul*, bound
up as it is with the life and sufferings of
centuries, entwined with memories sad,
rare, and glorious, a monument of the past
transported into the newer, better present,
a link between what has gone before and
what is.

A few minutes' walk down the street to
the right leads to the great cemetery, the
home of the dead. The graves are three
and four deep, and, therefore, the top of
the mounds is much higher than the street
without, and the floor of the synagogue
next to the graveyard lies many feet lower
than the cemetery. The tombstones are
very close together; some are beginning
to crumble, the inscriptions on others are
still very legible; the epitaphs have all
been copied, and a list of the Jewish families of Prague made in accordance with
the information gleaned from these silent
witnesses. The cemetery, known as the
Judengarten, "the Jews' garden," was ac-

quired for this purpose in the reign of Ottokar II, in 1254. The oldest tomb-stones were destroyed in the terrible per-secution of 1389, when the mob, in its fury, did not spare even the resting-places of the dead. The oldest existing epitaph dates from the year 1439.[85] Above the entrance to the cemetery one reads the inscription in Hebrew and German :

> " Reverence for antiquity ;
> Respect for ownership ;
> Rest for the dead."

This inscription dates from the year 1837, and finds its explanation in the fol-lowing circumstance : in that year the Jews of the city, finding their quarters too crowded, petitioned the town council to give them permission to live outside the Ghetto. The council concluded to grant the Jews permission to devote the ground of the old cemetery, not employed as a burial-place for over forty years, to build-ing purposes, and in this manner enlarge the Jewish quarter. In consequence of this, Rabbi Samuel Landau had the in-scription placed at the entrance. Needless to say, the permission of the council was not taken advantage of, and the cemetery not disturbed.

As one wanders among the graves, most of them old, centuries old, thought cannot but revert to the past and the checkered history of the Jews. Everything is quiet and peaceful now in this home of the dead, the troubled are at rest ; but as we read the names chiseled in the tombstones, some of celebrities who shed glory upon the Jewish community of Prague, most of them unknown or forgotten, we see pass before us the changing views of the panorama of bygone days, depicting scenes in which those resting here, the great and the small, the rich and the poor, the learned and the ignorant, were the actors. Most of the tombstones are plain slabs, but some over the graves of noted individuals are pretentious monuments. On many of the stones we note engraved figures, symbolical either of the class to which the deceased belonged, or of his condition, or his name. For instance, the tombstones of the Aaronides, i. e., of priestly families, are

adorned with two spreading hands, the
fingers in pairs, adjusted in the peculiar
way in which the priests held their hands
over the people while reciting the benedic-
tion. The stone erected over the grave
of a descendant of the Levites is marked
with a pitcher cut into the stone, while
that placed over the resting place of the
Israelite who can trace his ancestry back
to neither priest nor Levite, is distinguished by a sculptured bunch of grapes.
Besides these there are many other symbolical figures ; for example, on the tombstone of a young girl a female figure
is at times seen ; on that marking the
grave of a young wife, a female figure
carrying a rose. The name that the deceased bore, if taken from some object
in the animal or vegetable kingdom, so
often the case among the Jews, *c. g.*,
Wolf, Baer, Rose, Vögele (bird), Taube
(pigeon), Blume (flower), Löwe (lion),
Veilchen (violet), may be learned from
the figures of these objects on the stones.
The inscriptions are, of course, in Hebrew,
and are a valuable source for the history

of the Jews. They have all been copied, and the more important edited.[86] In this cemetery of Prague rest celebrated rabbis, renowned scholars, great physicians, noted philanthropists, men and women who in life did their duty well, and in death are not forgotten. Here one reads the epitaph of Mordecai Meisel (1528—1601), the great philanthropist, who paved the whole Jewish quarter, built two synagogues, the so-called *Hoch-Synagoge*, adjoining the *Rathhaus*, and the Meisel *Synagoge*, erected an almshouse, a school, a bath, did untold private charity, and assisted Jewish congregations elsewhere. Here, too, is the grave of Rabbi Judah ben Bezalel, known as the *Hohe Rabbi Löw*, about whose memory innumerable legends float. The people looked upon him as a magician, and the *Josefstadt* of to-day is still replete with traditions of his wonderful powers. Notable among these stories is that of the Homunculus (known among the Jews as the *Golem*), the figure created by him that attended to all his needs. The foundation for these stories

8

appears to be that he busied himself with scientific experiments. The contents of his interview with Emperor Rudolph, in 1592, never became known, hence it was made the basis of a legend. He was the most celebrated of the chief rabbis of Prague. The house in which he lived is still pointed out, and is marked with a sign, a lion on a blue background. As we pass along, we note the grave of David Gans (1541—1613), the historian, whose book, *Zemach David*, "The Sprout of David," is a chronicle of Jewish events from the creation to the year 1592 ; also that of the chief rabbi, David Oppenheim (1664—1736), who gathered that great collection of Hebrew books and manuscripts still designated by scholars as the *Bibliotheca Oppenheim*, the pride of the Bodleian library at Oxford, where it is now preserved intact ; of Joseph del Medigo, of Candia (1591—1655), one of the most renowned of Jewish scholars—physician, mathematician, philosopher and traveler, pupil of the great Galileo, and physician in ordinary of Prince Radziwill. Not far away rest the

remains of the noble man spoken of
above, Mordecai Zemach Kohen, through
whose almost superhuman efforts the decree of expulsion issued by Emperor Ferdinand was revoked. Near by is a pretentious monument, erected in memory of
one of the noblest and most charitable of
women, Hendel, wife of Jacob Bassewi von
Treuenberg, ennobled by Emperor Ferdinand II, in 1622 ; and so might many others
be named, who, in the old God's acre,
sleep the last earthly sleep, and who, in
their day, rose far above mediocrity. Only
a few of the most renowned have been
mentioned. A century has passed since
the last interment took place. A relic of
the past, the old cemetery remains quiet
and undisturbed by the troubled life of
the present. Its epitaphs, in their stony
silence, are eloquent witnesses of the
doings and ambitions of men and ages
gone, and as we step beyond its portal, we
feel that we are leaving the centuries of
persecution and oppression, and are going
out into the light of freedom. Of the significance and importance of these epi-

taphs, the great master of Jewish research says :[87]

"The epitaphs were intended to keep alive the memory of the dead unto posterity beyond the time in which the pious affection of relatives and admirers erected them, and the possession or knowledge of these inscriptions, though they reach no further back than the eleventh century, would have an incalculable value in increasing our meager information concerning Jewish families, as well as for literature and history. But nothing was destroyed and uprooted with colder indifference or with more bigoted fanaticism than the Jewish tombstones ; whatever tombstones of an old date existed in numberless places in Europe, Asia and Africa, were either purposely destroyed, or carelessly permitted to disappear. As a matter of course, the purchased sepulchers, together with the epitaphs, were the property of individuals, and the cemeteries acquired from princes, towns and bishops for large sums of money were the possessions of the congregations ; in spite of this the graves were

desecrated and plundered in the thirteenth
century in Spain, Italy, France, Germany.
'The sacred stones were thrown upon the
streets as an insult, the remains of those
who had worshipped God were removed
from their graves, and before the eyes of
the living the bodies of the dead were
trampled upon and plundered' (old prayer);
or after the expulsion and killing of the
Jews, the graveyards were seized, the
tombstones broken to pieces, and used for
other purposes. Throughout Germany,
between the fourteenth and the sixteenth
century, walls, foundations, churches and
houses were constructed with Jewish tombstones thus acquired."

So stands still the old Jewish quarter of
Prague ; its walls have fallen, the Jews have
scattered into all quarters of the city beyond its precincts, but still we thread the
narrow, crooked streets, and there crowd
in upon us thoughts, sad and painful, when
we recall the awful scenes here enacted,
and at the same time we are thrilled with
admiration for the constancy, heroism and
bravery of the thousands of Jews in the

dark years and centuries, in which they
withstood all the horrors to which they
were continually subjected. But through
the darkness that overhangs the past
gleams a bright light. In the narrow
lanes and byways, here and elsewhere,
grew up that beautiful Jewish home life
that has been one of the means of salvation for the Jews. The story of this life is
not recorded, but it is more important
than the outer events and misfortunes that
historians have made note of. By it the
character of the people was formed, and
as we look upon the unsightly houses in
the Jewish quarter, the wretched exterior
seems to float away, and the home scenes
of joy and love and religious constancy
shine brilliantly forth—perpetual lamps—
and explain how, in spite of woe and
misery, such as have fallen to the lot of no
other people so long and so continuously,
the Jews have found strength to live and
hope on. Religion and home, faith and
love, conviction and affection, these are
undying possessions that the Jews clung
to and preserved. The evils of the

Ghetto, a hideous nightmare, have passed; the things that imbued the long-suffering with strength, live forever. The mists dissolve, the sun-light spreads, wrong disappears, the just conquers, God reigns, and right must triumph.

CHAPTER VI.

THE GHETTO OF ROME.

The Jewish community of Rome is undoubtedly the oldest in Europe. The Jews
have lived there uninterruptedly since Pompey's time, probably even from an earlier
day,[88] with the possible exception of a
short period during the reign of Claudius,
who is said to have expelled them from
the city.[89] We have no notice that they
were compelled to leave the city at any
other time. Even during the terrible days
of the crusades, the Jews of Rome were
little affected by the cruelty of the mobs,
who inflicted untold sufferings on their
co-religionists in Germany, France, Austria and Bohemia. Their condition in imperial and papal Rome was usually bearable, for, in many instances, the popes were

kind, although there were occupants of the see of St. Peter who did all in their power to harass, humiliate and oppress them. Their residence of two thousand years in Rome, the center of Christianity, under conditions most unfavorable and depressing, is nothing short of a miracle. It is the same miracle that the preservation of Israel everywhere presents; it belongs to the scheme of Divine Providence. The people has a mission, and until that mission is fulfilled, it will continue to exist, whatever the external conditions and evils it must endure.

In the old imperial days, the Jews were confined to no special quarter; they could dwell anywhere in the city, although the majority lived in Transtiberis[90] (Transtevere), where their synagogue was situated. This portion of the city some of them continued to inhabit until the institution of the official Ghetto in 1556. But long before this time Jews lived on the left bank of the Tiber.[91] The bridge Quattro Capi was known as the *Pons Judæorum*, "bridge of the Jews." A

charter given in 1019 by Pope Benedict VIII to the bishopric of Portus, whose
jurisdiction extended over the island of
the Tiber and Transtevere, mentions, as
belonging to this territory, *fundum integ-
rum, qui vocatur Judæorum,* "the whole
district, named after the Jews," and designates, as its boundary, *medium pontem ubi
Iudæi habitare videntur,* "the middle of
the bridge, where the Jews appear to
dwell."[92]

Their papal masters were content to
permit the Jews to live as they had been
accustomed for centuries. With papal legislation in regard to the Jews we are not
concerned here, except in so far as it touched
their dwelling place. With this none of
the popes, the spiritual and temporal masters of Rome, interfered until the time of
the cruel Paul IV Caraffa, one of the
most sinister pontiffs that ever occupied
the see of St. Peter. He was the one to
institute torture chambers and the censor-
ship in Rome. He was hated alike by
Christians and Jews. So bitter was the
animosity against him, that upon his death

the Roman people execrated and cursed his memory. They applauded a Jew who placed a yellow hat upon his statue, and thereupon the people dragged the statue through the streets of Rome to the Capitol, destroyed it, and threw the head with the hat into the Tiber. This man, whom the Jews designated by the name of Israel's traditional arch-enemy, Haman, has the sorry renown[93] of having established the Roman Ghetto, into which, for three hundred years, thousands of human creatures were crowded, a disgrace to humanity and civilization. Scarce had he ascended the papal throne when, on July 12, 1555, he promulgated the famous bull, *Cum nimis absurdum*, in reference to the Jews. It repeats all the restrictions to which the Jews were accustomed, but the only portion that interests us here is the command that "in Rome and all other cities of the Papal States the Jews shall live entirely separated from the Christians, in a quarter or a street with one entrance and one exit; they shall have but one synagogue, shall build no

new synagogue, nor own real estate." In
spite of petition and protest, the Jews of
Rome were forced into their prison. Paul
IV designated as the Ghetto a small
territory consisting of a few narrow, unhealthy streets along the left bank of
the Tiber, and extending from the bridge
Quattro Capi to the Via del Pianto,
"the street of lamentation." Truly, an ap-
propriate entrance for the new quarter, as it
was a place of lamentation for the Jews, and
with weeping and wailing they entered it
on July 26, 1556. The Jews resisted at
the start; one of them, David d'Ascoli,
published a pamphlet setting forth the
reasons why his co-religionists should not
be treated thus; for his pains he was condemned to imprisonment for life.

At first the district was named *vicus
Judæorum*, later Ghetto. It was shut in
by gates. Paul IV has been called the
"heartless Pharaoh, who exposed the Jews
to all the ills bound to arise from the
cramped space and the low situation of
the dwellings along the river, and these
ills were a host of Egyptian plagues." For

example, in 1656, the Ghetto became such
a hotbed of infection that the gates were
closed for·three months, and the unhappy
inhabitants were not permitted to leave
the quarter during all that time. A
traveler of forty years ago speaks as follows of the Ghetto: "When I visited it
(the Ghetto) the first time, the Tiber had
just overflowed its banks, and the yellow
flood flowed through the Fiumara, the
lowest street of the Ghetto, the foundations of the houses of which stand partly
in the water; the river also coursed along
the Octavia (another street), and covered
the lower portions of the lowest houses.
What a melancholy sight to see the wretched Jewish quarter thus sunk in the waves
of the Tiber! Yearly must Israel in Rome
experience the deluge, and the Ghetto
survives the flood, like Noah's ark, with
human creatures and animals. The danger increases, when the Tiber, swelled by
rains, is driven back from the sea by west
winds; then all who live in the lower
stories of the houses must seek refuge in
the upper apartments."[91]

An Italian writer, in discoursing upon
the emancipation of the Jews in 1848, describes this Ghetto as a "formless heap of
hovels and dirty cottages, ill kept, in
which a population of nearly four thousand souls vegetates, when half that number could with difficulty live there. The
narrow, unclean streets, the scarcity of
fresh air, and the filth, inevitable consequences of such a conglomeration of human
beings, wretched for the most part, render
this hideous dwelling place nauseous and
deadly."[95]

This squalid quarter the Jews had to
occupy, and the inhumanity of Paul IV
placed the capstone upon the column of
indignity, erected in the course of the
Christian centuries, block upon block, each
designating some new disgrace heaped
upon the Jews. Unrelenting was Paul
IV in his inimical attitude towards the devoted people, and the day of his death
was hailed with joy throughout the Jewry
of the Papal States, the Jews hoping that,
as each new pope was an independent
sovereign, and made new rules for the

government of his state, his successor
might revoke his decrees. That was the
only comfort that the Jews had whenever
a specially unfriendly pope occupied St.
Peter's: possibly his successor would be
kind to them. And in this hope they were
justified this time. Pius IV (1559—1565),
the successor of Caraffa, entertained kindlier sentiments toward the Jews. He lightened their burden considerably, and his
treatment was a great relief from the
unremitting and unrelaxing cruelty of his
predecessor. In 1561, at the urgent request of the Jews, he issued a brief to the
Jews of the Papal States, of the following
import : His predecessor had promulgated
a bull regulating the life of the Jews, which
some, out of desire for their riches, had
made use of to harass them. He, therefore,
decreed that the Jews, on their journeys,
might put aside the yellow head-covering,
and that they be obliged to wear it only
in the places in which they staid longer
than one day ; that, if the quarter assigned
to them in the cities was insufficient for
them and their business, it could be en-

larged by the governor or vice-legate, or
a larger and more fitting quarter could be
assigned to them ; that they could acquire,
besides their houses in these quarters,
other property to the value of 1500 gold
ducats ; that they could rent this property
to Christians, could do business with Christians, could exercise all trades, deal in all
manner of goods, and have intercourse
with Christians, but not employ Christian
servants ; that, in the quarters assigned to
them (viz., the Ghetto, established by Paul
IV), the (Christian) owners of the houses
could not ask exorbitant rents, but had to
rent the houses at a price determined by
the executive of the city. There were
many other regulations in this favorable
decree, but the last mentioned was of especial importance. At the accession of
Pius V (1566—1572), the next pope, the sky
was again overclouded for the Jewish resi-
dents of Rome. The mildness of Pius IV
had given them some respite, and encour-
aged them to hope for better things, but in
the days of Pius V the spirit of Paul IV was
revived. He revoked the concessions of

his immediate predecessor, and renewed the harsh bull of Paul IV, *Cum nimis absurdum.* The Jews, when ordered to the Ghetto, had been commanded to sell all their real estate outside. They had evaded this, and in the time of Pius IV, as noted above, they had again been permitted to acquire landed property. Pius V, however, ordered, in reference to this matter, that all property owned by the Jews not sold within a specified time, or sold only on pretense, was to become the possession of the church. In 1569, he ordered the Jews of all cities and towns of the Papal States, with the exception of Rome and Ancona, to leave within three months under pain of slavery and confiscation of their possessions. The Jews of these two cities were commanded not to harbor the exiles, and were forbidden to leave their own city to go to another place. He also laid down specific regulations for the Jews of the Roman Ghetto. Every Jew had to be in the Ghetto by nightfall. After the *Ave Maria*, the gates of the Ghetto were to be closed. Any Jew who was

9

caught outside after nightfall, was punished severely, unless he succeeded in
bribing the watchman. Gregory XIII
(1572—1585), the next pope, legislated in
much the same spirit, but it is said that he
permitted the Jews whom Pius V had expelled from the Papal States to return[96].

Sixtus V (1585—1590),possibly the most
humane and liberal minded of all the occupants of the papal see, followed him.
He was very kindly disposed toward the
Jews, and in his day matters looked
brighter for them than they had dared
hope. In 1586 he issued his bull, *Chris-
tiana pietas*, in which he gave the Jews
permission to settle in all cities of his domain, and suitable dwellings at the customary rents were to be assigned to them.
These rents were not to be raised later.
In places where they had had synagogues
formerly, they were permitted to re-open
them. In short, in this bull, he renewed
all the privileges of the Jews. In his
time, attracted by the leniency of his rule,
many Jews came to Rome to live.

Clement VIII (1592—1605) issued his

bull, *Cæca et perfidia Hebræorum obdu-
rata*, on February 25, 1593. He revoked
the mild decrees of Pius IV and Sixtus V,
and put into force again the harsh regulations of Paul IV and Pius V. He again
expelled all the Jews who had returned to
the cities of the Papal States during the
pontificate of Sixtus V. Within three
months of the date of the publication of
the bull, all the Jews except those of
Rome, Ancona and Avignon, permitted to
remain because of the large commercial
interests in their hands, again had to
leave their homes. The Jews in Bologna
at that time numbered nine hundred souls.
On their departure from the city, with that
filial reverence characteristic of the Jews,
they took the bones of their dead with
them, and re-interred them in the cemetery at Piere di Cento, where there was a
small Jewish congregation.

When Paul IV assigned the quarter between the Via del Pianto and the Ponte
del Quattro Capi to the Jews as their
Ghetto, Christian families were living in
that region. They had to move out of their

homes, of which, of course, they retained
the ownership ; many of the other houses
were also owned by Christians. These
houses the Jews had to rent. They had
no alternative. They *had* to live there.
The landlords, knowing this, could ask almost any sum, and they were not slow in
taking advantage of the situation. The
Jews, having been forced into this dwelling place, had to be protected in some manner from extortionate rents and from the
whim of the landlord, who might put them
out at any moment. So it was found necessary in the time of Clement VIII to
issue the law regulating the holding of
property in the Ghetto and the relation of
tenant to landlord, a law that remained in
force until the abolition of the Ghetto.
This law was to the effect that the Roman
owners should remain in possession of the
houses, but the Jewish tenants were to be
given a leasehold ; they could not be
given notice to move so long as they paid
their rent. The rent, fixed by the authorities, could not be raised. The Jew could
change and enlarge the house if he de-

sired. This right was given a special name, the *jus gazzaga* (from the Hebrew *chazakah*, meaning right of possession), and everyone who held such a lease valued it highly, since it assured him and his family of a roof over their heads, and protected him from the wanton treatment of grasping landlords. This *jus gazzaga* was handed down in families from generation to generation, and they who possessed it were regarded as remarkably fortunate,— fortunate to be assured of the right of dwelling in a close, confined, miserable corner of the city! But the Jew had to be thankful not only for a dwelling place, but for the mere right to live.

In reference to this *jus gazzaga*, or possession of leaseholds of the houses in the Ghetto, Alexander VII (1655—1667) issued a decree favorable to converted Jews. The popes made continual efforts to convert the Jews by every method in their power, as will be noticed later on. At times they succeeded, and naturally these converted Jews were not regarded with the most affectionate feelings by their

former brethren in faith. Now, it happened
at times that a converted Jew was in possession of a *jus gazzaga.* He, of course,
could move out of the Ghetto, and live
wherever he desired ; that was one of the
inducements held out for conversion.
Thereby his house in the Ghetto, of which
he held the perpetual lease, became va-
cant, and he was anxious to rent it, since
he had to pay rent to the Roman owner.
The Jews, however, banded themselves
together, and agreed not to rent such
houses, in order to injure the faithless and
keep others from accepting Christianity.
Alexander, therefore, issued a brief in
1657, to the effect that the Jews of the
Ghetto, as a community, had to make
good the rent of such houses as long as
they stood empty. In 1658 he issued a
further decree in regard to the *jus gazzaga.* Since the Jews, without the knowledge of the owners of the houses, often
sold this *jus* on burdensome conditions ;
since they made contracts and gave mortgages on it, so that it became difficult for
the owners to collect their rents ; since

they took undertenants into the houses, by
whom the property was ruined, the owners incurring the cost of repair; since
they often left houses arbitrarily, and
mutually agreed that no Jew should rent
certain ones, the pope issued the same law
as in regard to the houses whose leaseholds were in the possession of converted
Jews, viz., the community of the Ghetto
had to pay the rent of such houses to the
landlords. Houses in the Ghetto were
valuable ; even when empty they filled the
coffers of their owners.

The story of the relations between the
popes and the Jews does not belong here,
except in so far as it especially affected the
community of Rome. The spiritual jurisdiction of the popes extended over the
whole Catholic world, and their repeated
decrees against Jewish books, the Talmud
in particular ; their dealings with the In-
quisition in its efforts to root out the secret Jews in Spain, Portugal and Italy ;
their edicts in regard to the attire of the
Jews ; the association of Jews with Christians ; the employment of Christian ser-

vants and nurses by Jews, and many other
laws of the same import affected the
Roman Ghetto only as a part of the community of European Jews. But there
were points in which the Jews of Rome
stood in special relations to the pope.

It has been stated that the popes were,
for the most part, kind masters, and that
the lot of the Jews in the papal capital
was better than elsewhere.[97] The Jews
of Rome escaped the terrible persecutions, the bloody massacres, the frightful accusations, the heartless expulsions
that mark the history of their brethren
in France, England, Germany, Spain,
Portugal and Austria. They were subjected to indignities, but to nothing more
serious. They were often molested, and
pettily persecuted ; they were made the
objects of scorn and mockery, not of
murder and pillage. Rome was frequently a place of refuge, and often received them when they were driven out
of other Italian states and other countries.
The clemency of many of the popes was
due to the fact that they were the tem-

poral rulers of the city, and whenever
their material interests clashed with the
spiritual legislation in regard to the Jews,
the former being the nearer concern obtained prime consideration.[95] The Jews
were useful citizens in times of need, and
often aided the popes with money in their
struggles with rival powers. As everywhere, the Jew's money was his weapon.
Up to the pontificate of Paul IV, their condition in Rome was bearable. Such popes
as Gregory the Great, Alexander III, Ho-
norius III, Gregory IX, Nicholas IV, were
really kind and benevolently disposed towards them. But from the day of Paul
IV, with the exceptions already noted, the
bull *Cum nimis absurdum* became the
charter of the Jews of Rome, "the pivot
upon which their life and history revolved."

Even before the official institution of
the Ghetto by Paul IV, it was customary
for the Jewish community of Rome to
assist in welcoming the new pope on his
entrance into the city. This entrance
resembled a triumphal march, and was, a
magnificent spectacle. The Jews did

homage to the new pope, and usually
from his reception of them they learned
whether the coming years would bring
weal or woe. The first mention of the
participation of the Jews in welcoming the
pope is in the time of Calixtus II, at
whose entrance in 1120 the plaudits of
the Jews mingled with those of the Romans. They usually met the pope with
the scroll of the Law. When Innocent
II, in 1138, entered Rome, the Jews approached him on his way to the Lateran
palace, bent the knee before him, and
handed their scroll to him in sign of homage. He answered, "We praise and
honor the Law, for it was given your
fathers by Almighty God through Moses.
But we condemn your cult and your false
interpretation of the Law, for you await
the Redeemer in vain; the apostolic faith
teaches us that our Lord Jesus Christ has
already appeared." When Eugenius III
entered upon the pontifical office in 1145,
Jews were present at the great celebration, carrying the Mosaic Law on their
shoulders. Alexander III, in 1165, was

received by a vast multitude, among them the Jews, carrying their Law in their arms according to custom. A great multitude of priests, laymen and Jews in 1187 accorded Clement III a hearty welcome amid songs and praises.[99] The method of the reception of the Jews was definitely fixed. In the description of the pope's welcome, we read in the *Ordo Romanus:* "And the Jews come with their Law, make obeisance, and offer him the Law for him to honor it, and then the pope commends the Law, and condemns the cult and interpretation of the Jews, because they say that the Redeemer will come, while the Church teaches and preaches that the Lord Jesus Christ has already come." The Jews on these occasions usually stood arrayed on the Monte Guardano, or at the Arch of Titus, which lay on the road of the pope to the Vatican. The Arch of Titus, one of the.most valued remains of antiquity, was erected after the conquest of Jerusalem by Titus. On its frieze is the figure of an old man on a bier, representing the river Jordan; on the arch itself are pictured the seven-branched golden candlestick, the golden table, the ark and the silver trumpets, all connected with the worship of the Temple. To the Jews this arch embodied the loss of their land. It seemed to them to bespeak their shame and humiliation, and no Jew of Rome ever passed through it; he always made a detour, and passed around the side.[100]

The Jews, standing in these public places, became the objects of scorn for the Roman populace; the *gamins* jeered and mocked them, the populace subjected them to insult and contumely. As a result of their request to be saved from this treatment, Innocent VIII permitted them in 1484 to appear in the inner space of the Castello St. Angelo. In 1513 Leo X received them at the gate of this castle. They reached him the Law for his confirmation. The pope took it, and said: *Confirmamus sed non consentimus,* "We confirm, but do not assent." This was the last time that this ceremony took place.

One of the greatest indignities to which

the Jews of Rome were subjected was their
compulsory participation in the races on
the Corso at the carnival. The populace
demanded as a great source of pleasure
that Jews run in the races. Paul II, in
1468, instituted these races, and amid the
gibes and jeers of the attendant crowds,
a number of Jews were forced annually to
participate ; their companions in the races
were asses, buffaloes and Barbary horses.
What rare sport it was for the Roman
populace to see the victims of their scorn
and contempt come forth, with no cover-
ing but a cloth about their loins, and run
the length of the Corso on an equal footing with animals ! The weak degraded
by the strong ! So was it always in Rome :
none too low, none too degraded to
consider himself above the wretched inhabitants of the Ghetto, whose very right
of residence depended on their doing the
will of their superiors. How the crowds
laughed and shouted with delight at the
sight of the Jews racing ! How the
Christians pointed the finger of scorn,
and noble and *gamin*, cardinal and beggar,

flung insult and contumely at the miserable
ones! Time and again the Jews begged
to be spared this disgrace, but for two
centuries they were forced to endure it,
and only in 1668 Clement IX lent a favorable ear to their entreaty, and granted
them the request to be freed from the
shame. In lieu of appearing on the race
course they paid 300 scudi yearly to the
papal treasury.

It was understood that the Jews lived
in Rome only on sufferance, and yearly
they had to perform the ceremony of
asking permission to dwell there another
year. On the first day of the carnival,
the heads of the Jewish community appeared before the council of the city as
a deputation from the Jews. They pros-
trated themselves, and presented a bouquet
and twenty scudi to be used in decorating
the balcony on which the Roman senate
sat during the carnival. This deputation
at the same time requested the senate to
permit the Jews to remain in Rome. A
senator placed his foot on the forehead of
the Jews, bade them rise, and told them,

in the words of a traditional formula, that the Jews were not taken into Rome as citizens, but were suffered in charity.[101] This humiliation, too, they were spared in 1847 by Pius IX, but in 1850 they still had to appear at the Capitol on the first day of the carnival to express their sub-mission, and pay a tribute of eight hun-dred scudi in remembrance of the favor that they were excused from taking part in the races and furnishing amusement to the people at this time.

One of the great objects of the popes was to convert the Jews to Christianity by any means whatsoever, since they firmly believed that by this they were accomplish-ing an important and holy work. From their standpoint, they looked upon the Jews as lost. They attributed the refusal to accept Christianity to obstinacy and blindness. Various methods were em-ployed by them, but the strangest of all was that introduced by Pope Gregory XIII at the instigation of a converted Jew, Joseph Tzarfati. In his bull, *Sancta mater ecclesia*, of September 1, 1584, he com-

manded that in all places where there was a
sufficient number of Jews, a sermon should
be preached to them on the truths of
Christianity every Saturday.[102]   This sermon was designated *predica coattiva.*   All
Jews above the age of twelve, unless prevented by sickness, or some other adequate
excuse to be given to the bishop, were to
attend, so that always at least one-third of
the Jewish population was to be present.   This was carried out in Rome, especially in the eighteenth century.   On
Saturday afternoon, the strange sight
of the police driving men, women, and
children over twelve to church with whips,
could be witnessed in the Roman Ghetto.
Saturday afternoon was chosen, because
it was thought that the words preached to
them in the church, setting forth the doctrines and truths of Christianity, compared
with the teachings of Judaism listened to
in the morning in the synagogue, would
appear so far superior and so much more
worthy of acceptance that they would
be converted easily.   At first one hundred and fifty had to appear, but the num-

ber was later made three hundred. At the entrance of the church stood a watchman, who counted those that entered to make sure that the number was full. In the church, the police made the people pay attention ; if anyone appeared inattentive, or under the soporific influence of the sermon fell asleep, he was aroused by blows of the whip. The preacher, usually a Dominican, took as his text some passage from the Bible read in the morning in the synagogue, and gave the Catholic interpretation. These services were first held in the church of San Benedetto alla Regola, afterwards in the church of San Angelo in Pescaria.[103] Needless to say, the effort proved entirely fruitless ; from a weekly it dropped into an occasional service, held five times a year. It was gradually dying out when Leo XII revived it in 1824, and it was finally abolished in 1847, the first year of Pius IX.

It was not due to lack of zeal on the part of the popes and the church that the Jews did not adopt Christianity. The greatest inducements were held out to converts :

10

they were released from the Ghetto, and
granted all civil rights and privileges.
Some converts, of course, there were, and
there can be no doubt that in the veins of
many bearing proud, old, Roman aristocratic names the blood of these converted Jews
flows. At the ceremony adopting a Jew into
Christianity, always performed with great
show and pomp, *ad majorem Dei et eccle-
siæ gloriam*, some member of the highest
aristocracy frequently stood sponsor, and
as in ancient Rome the client took the name
of his patrician patron, so here the converted Jew took that of his aristocratic
sponsor.[104]   His descendants are known
by that name, and are looked upon as a
branch of that noble family.   As a constant reminder of their obduracy in not
accepting Christianity, there was, opposite
the Ghetto, on a chapel near the bridge
Quattro Capi, a picture of the crucifixion
with the verse Isaiah LXV, 2: "I spread out
my hands all the time unto a rebellious people, that walk in the way which is not
good."   The unremitting efforts at conversion met with partial success.   A num-

ber of Jews adopted Christianity in
order to improve their lot in life, and
the careers of some of these apostates
and their descendants are so brilliant,
striking and surprising that they may well
excite wonder. I mention one, because
of the strange fact that a descendant of
the despised Jews rose to the highest
position in the Catholic world, a sufficient
excuse for introducing a short account of
his career. It is stated in various accounts
that the anti-pope Anacletus II, who maintained himself against Innocent II and the
greater portion of the Catholic clergy,
was of Jewish descent.[105] Anacletus was
supported in his claim by the Romans,
Sicilians and Milanese. He compelled his
rival to flee from Rome twice, and maintained his position until the 'time of his
death, in the year 1138. The following account of Anacletus and his family will
leave no room for doubt as to his Jewish
origin :

In the eleventh and twelfth centuries the
Roman Jewish family Pierleoni acquired
great riches, and having become converted

to Christianity, played a great rôle in Rome
and in the church. The anti-pope Anacletus II (1130—1138), the cause of much
dissension in Rome and in the church, was
a scion of this family.[106] About the middle
of the eleventh century, Benedict, the head
of the family, was baptized, and married a
lady of the Roman nobility. His son, Leo,
and his grandson, Peter Leon, with whom
the name Pierleoni begins, belonged to the
grandees of Rome ; they also bore the
title of consul. They had built their
castle at the entrance of the Ghetto,
next to the bridge leading to the island of
the Tiber, and this island was ruled by
them ; even the tower of the Crescent
was intrusted to them by Pope Urban II in
1098. In the struggle between the popes
and the emperors regarding the investi-
ture, they always took the part of the popes.
Urban II had died in 1099, in the castle of
Leo, the leader of the papal party, the only
place where he had felt secure. Leo's son,
Peter, in the name of Pope Pascal II, con-
ducted the negotiations regarding the in-
vestiture with Emperor Henry V, before

his coronation in 1110. He died in 1128, and
one epitaph extols his piety, while another
praises him "as a man unexcelled in riches
and glory."[107] He had sought to procure for one of his sons the highly important office of prefect of the city, but
had failed because a powerful party was
opposed to him. One of his daughters
became the wife of King Roger, of Sicily,
and another son, also named Peter, first
appeared as a monk in Cluny. Then through
the efforts of his father he became cardinal, and finally, in the year 1130, he was
chosen anti-pope with the appellation Anacletus II. According to contemporary
writers, whose testimony, however, must
be used with much care, this family never
entirely lost its Jewish type, either physically or mentally.[108] These writers also say
that with keen foresight they ranged themselves on the side of the reform popes, and
acquired the highest political influence.
The ancestor of the family had amassed
an immense fortune by money transactions,
and the rest followed in his footsteps. His
numerous descendants intermarried largely

with the Roman grandees. The remainder of the nobility, however, hated
them as upstarts.

The picture which these chroniclers
draw of Anacletus is not very flattering.
No doubt they were influenced by a parti-
san spirit, as they were all strongly in
favor of Innocent, his rival.[109] One reports
that Peter, the father of the pope, had
the reputation of being an execrable
usurer, and was, therefore, most bitterly
hated. Walter, archbishop of Ravenna,
calls the schism of Anacletus a "heresy
of Jewish perfidy." St. Bernard com-
plains that a descendant of the Jews oc-
cupies the chair of Peter, and that this is
an affront to Christ. Another designates
him as an avaricious and inordinately ambitious man. Innocent II, the rival
claimant to the papal throne, himself
wrote to Emperor Lothair, who sided
with him, that Peter Leon, *i. e.*, Anacletus, had been striving for the papal crown
for a long time, and had obtained possession of it by means of violence, bloodshed
and robbery; that he imprisoned pilgrims

who came from a distance to visit the
graves of the apostles, and tortured them
by every means, hunger, thirst, etc.
Innocent, in a letter to Hugo, Archbishop
of Rouen, also calls the action of Anacletus "insane Jewish perfidy."[110]

Anacletus died on the 25th of January,
1138. His relatives buried him quietly in
an unknown spot.[111] Shortly thereafter
they, with all their adherents, submitted
to Innocent.

Evidently this anti-pope was neither
better nor worse than the great majority of
the occupants of the papal chair of that
time. If contemporary writers may be
believed, he employed every means to
compass his ends. In one point they all
seem to be agreed, viz., that he was of
Jewish descent, and this, as a matter of
course, made him much more despicable
in their eyes than all the deeds of violence. His career furnishes a very interesting episode in the history of the
Jews of Rome.

A few words more on the subject of
conversions. There were houses or homes

for catechumens, a monastery for males, a
convent for females, where all such Jews as
were in the least likely to be converted were
kept, taught and supported until the time
of their conversion. If he had once consented, by word or sign, to adopt Christianity, there was no possibility for the
Jew to retract. There are many instances on record of men and women,
who, regretting their resolve, desired to
return to the Jewish community before
their conversion, but were not permitted;
some met death, others imprisonment, as
a result of their constancy. The affirma-
tion of a witness, that he had heard a Jew
express the intention to adopt Christianity,
a remark dropped in conversation, a ges-
ture, was considered evidence sufficient,
and the papal police were sent into the
Ghetto to seize the candidate, to search
for him if he could not be found at once, and
to bring him into the house of the catechumens by force, if necessary."[2] The following two instances illustrate the methods
employed: "On the 5th of May, 1605,
Stella, the daughter of Jacob, was brought

into the convent, because one of her relatives, a catechumen, affirmed that, in his
hearing, she had expressed the wish to become a Christian. After resisting for
twenty-five days, she consented to abjure
her faith. She was baptized under the
name of Hortense."[113]

" On April 26, 1689, upon the declara-
tion of two witnesses, the protector of the
catechumens sent some soldiers into the
Ghetto to seize a young girl nineteen
years old. The Jews hid her; her mother
and brother were arrested, and the young
girl had to surrender herself. She did not
renounce Judaism until the fifth day of
the following January."[114]

It was with children that the conver-
sionists scored their greatest success. If
a Christian took a Jewish child in the
absence of its parents, and had it baptized,
it was considered a *bona fide* conversion.
In spite of the protests of the parents,
the tears of the mother, the agony of the
father, their child was kept from them, and
raised as a Christian, and the parents perhaps never saw it more. The Mortara

case, in this century, was typical of many
that occurred in the zeal for converting
Jews. Any means were considered legitimate.

Intercourse between the catechumen
and his co-religionists was forbidden
under penalty of the whipping-post and a
fine of twenty-five crowns; this prohibition included entering the Ghetto, eating,
drinking, sleeping with Jews, or even
speaking to them. A catechumen appre-
hended in conversation with his own
father or mother was severely punished
either by fine, bastinado or exile.

After the catechumen had expressed
his readiness to accept the faith, the sac-
raments were administered to him on
some feast day, either Epiphany or Pen-
tecost. Usually the pope himself was
present; the presiding cardinal addressed
the multitude at length upon the miracle
about to take place; thereupon the convert, clothed in white satin, was led
through the streets of the city in a car-
riage, that the citizens might be edified by
the sight, and everybody might attest the

conversion. If the convert was married,
his conversion annulled his Jewish marriage, and he could wed a Christian without
ado. There was in Rome a society, the
Brotherhood of St. Joseph, whose especial
object it was to convert Jews ; this brotherhood was favored greatly by the popes.
Large resources were required to further
its work and to support the houses of the
catechumens. Whence obtain the funds?
What portion of the community should be
taxed to carry on the holy work of converting Jews? Who was benefited more by
these saintly proceedings than Jews themselves? Therefore, let the Jewish communities be taxed for this purpose. Truly,
a brilliant thought! The Jews themselves
were to furnish the sinews of war for the
proselytizing campaigns of Christianity
among their own. Julius III, in his bull,
Pastoris æterni vices, of August 31, 1554,
was the first to impose this tax ; ten florins
per synagogue was the quota he named.
Later, this was increased greatly, and in
the period from 1565 to 1568 ten Jewish
communities of Italy were compelled to
contribute 5238 crowns for this purpose.[115]

The most active proselytizing zeal of
the popes with regard to the Jews coin-
cides with the period of the Protestant
Reformation, as though they wished to
offset the losses occasioned by the lapses
from Catholicism to Protestantism by ac-
cessions from the Jews.

Vain hope! not all the promises of
favor succeeded in compassing that end in
more than a slight degree. Amid all the
horrors of the Ghetto, the great majority
of the Jews remained true to their inherited
faith even though renunciation meant the
enjoyment of all the rights and benefits of
which, as Jews, they were deprived.

In 1712, Clement XI transferred the
property and the privileges of the Brotherhood of St. Joseph, the fraternity that
exercised care and protection over the
catechumens, to the *Pii Operai*,[116] who continued the work, but at present their
activity as agents for the conversion of
the Jews has well nigh ceased.[117]

The Jewish community of Rome, although under the jurisdiction of the popes,
was still, in a measure, autonomous. Nat-

urally, Jewish life centred in the synagogue. This was situated in the Piazza
di Scuola or Temple Court. The building consisted of five synagogues combined, the Catalonian, the Sicilian, the
Castilian, the New Synagogue and the
Temple proper.[118] In all likelihood, they
received their names from the different
rituals used, and were probably founded by
exiles from various countries who sought
refuge in Rome. These synagogues,
though virtually distinct, were all united
into one building, because the Jews were
not permitted to have more than one
house of worship. The structure was destroyed by fire in the winter of 1893, and
many valuable relics were consumed in
the flames. All the *débris* of prayer books,
Bibles, etc., rescued from the fire was buried
in the cemetery, and a memorial stone is
to be erected over the spot.

The Jewish community of Rome was
looked up to by the other Italian Jewish
communities as having a certain pre-emi-
nence. The rabbi's influence was prepon-
derating. The executive heads of the com-

munity were the three *fattori;* they regu-
lated the taxes, and superintended the
weekly distribution of alms to the poor.
They were held responsible by the pope
for the good order of the Ghetto. 'The
legislative body of the Ghetto was the
council of sixty; its duty was the regulation of the internal life of the Ghetto; it
named the officers, chose the rabbi, and
exercised the right of excommunication.
As may be readily understood, its power
was only advisory. Its decisions had to
be sanctioned by the papal officer who had
jurisdiction over the Ghetto.

The edict of Pius VI issued on April 5,
1775, remains to be mentioned. It has
been termed "the blackest page in the
history of mankind."[9] It consisted of
forty-four paragraphs, and repeated, in the
harshest manner, all the old restrictive
legislation in reference to Jews. The
thirty-seventh paragraph may be given
here as the last official expression bearing
upon our subject :

" Jews of both sexes may not live outside
of the Ghettos. They may not sojourn in

villages, on country estates, in castles, parks or anywhere else on any pretext whatsoever, not even on the plea that they require change of air, and if they require such change, and they wish to go away and remain even one day, they must be particular—according to the decree of the holy assembly of May 19, 1751, agreeing with a like decree of Alexander VII, of September 6, 1661—to secure a written permission in which must be contained the name, the surname and the descent of the Jew, the legal ground upon which the permission was granted him, the length of time of its validity, together with the conditions that the Jews must wear the sign on the hat as is directed above in Article 20, and that they may not live with Christians, nor associate with them in friendly companionship. Upon return, they shall give back the permit to the court from which they received it under pain of a fine of three hundred scudi, imprisonment and other discretional penalties for every act of disobedience."

The inhumanity that breathes in this

decree is characteristic of the whole edict.
The saturnine spirit of Paul IV lived again
in Pius VI. But temporary relief at least
was coming for the victims of centuries of
persecution. In 1798, Pius VI, after the
occupation of Rome by the army of the
French Republic, left the city never to
return. The Roman Republic was pro-
claimed. The Jews profited by the new
state of things. Although the French occupied the city a little less than two years,
and later the old condition of affairs was
in part re-established, yet one of the greatest indignities to which the Jews had been
subjected was abolished at this time. On
July 9, 1798, the distinguishing mark that
the Jews had been forced to wear was
officially abolished by an edict of General
St. Cyr.

In 1800, the new pope, Pius VII, entered Rome. He evinced kindly feeling
toward his Jewish subjects, although he
did nothing effectual to improve their condition. In 1808 the French again occupied Rome. The pope was led away a
prisoner. The affairs of the Jews were

taken in hand by the French. They were given equal rights with all citizens. The gates of the Ghetto were not locked at night. They were granted permission to carry on any trade. This meant a great deal, for Innocent XIII, in renewing Paul IV's infamous bull, had added thereto, in 1724, the restriction that the Jews of Rome be permitted to ply no trade but that of dealing in old clothes, rags and iron. A few years later, in 1740, Benedict XIV extended this by allowing them to deal also in new clothes. Their freedom, however, lasted but a short time. Pius VII returned to Rome in 1814 after the departure of the French. Although the new regulations that had been instituted by the French were annulled, yet the condition of affairs was an improvement upon what it had been before the French invasion. The pope permitted the Jews to open stores in the vicinity of the Ghetto outside of its walls. A small number of families were also permitted to live outside of the Ghetto.

His successor, Leo XII (1823—1829),

11

gave the Jews the right to acquire houses
over and beyond those covered by the *jus
gazzaga*. He increased the number of
the gates of the Ghetto to eight, which
were closed every night. He legislated for
the most part in the old spirit, and many of
the more prominent families emigrated
from Rome to other lands, where Jews
enjoyed greater freedom. The next popes,
Pius VIII (1829—1830), and Gregory
XVI (1831—1846), did nothing for the bet-
termemt of the lot of their Jewish subjects.

But even Rome had to pay regard to
the spirit of liberation and emancipation
abroad everywhere in Europe, and, in
1847, the new pope, Pius IX, who had
lately ascended the papal throne, determined to have the gates and walls of the
Ghetto destroyed, and to permit the Jews
to dwell anywhere in the city. On the
eve of Passover, April 17, 1848, strange
sounds were heard by the Jews, who were
celebrating their feast. Often in the
past had sounds and noises on that night
struck terror to the hearts of the Jewish
inhabitants of more than one Ghetto. But

too frequently on this occasion had enemies and excited mobs accused them of having murdered a Christian to use his blood at
their feast. Faces blanched and limbs
trembled, for the poor creatures knew
well what misery and trouble that lie
always bore in its train.[120] For once, the
sounds from without on the Passover eve
bore a joyful message. The purpose of
demolishing the walls of the Ghetto had
been kept a secret from the Jews of Rome,
and when they learned the import of the
blows that resounded in the night, what
joy, what happiness was theirs! At last
the walls of the Ghetto were removed,
and they were free men like all others!
But their joy was not of long duration.
The policy of Pius IX was liberal in
the first two years of his reign, but a
reactionary movement set in after the
revolutions of 1848, and the Ghetto was re-
established. For twenty-two years longer,
despite the removal of Ghettos everywhere, it continued to stand, a reproach
to the city. In 1870, the Jews themselves
took the matter in hand, and prepared a

remarkable petition, begging for the abolition of the Ghetto, and setting forth their
sad plight. The opening portion of this
important document (first published a few
years ago),[121] which graphically describes
the horrors of the Ghetto and the misery
of its inhabitants, may properly find a
place here. The Jews of Rome addressed
the ruler under whose power they lived,
and in whose mercy they trusted, as follows :

" Most Holy Father ! The elders and
the delegates of the Jewish community of
Rome, faithful subjects of your Holiness,
prostrate themselves before your exalted
throne, and offer the assurance of the
continued loyalty of their co-religionists.
This feeling of loyalty is the result of the
many conspicuous deeds of kindness which
we, O Holy Father, have experienced at
your hands, and we are now animated by
the pleasant sensation of hope, since your
exalted will has consented to receive new
petitions in its name. In fulfilment of the
duty imposed on them, the petitioners
presume humbly and reverently to lay be-

fore your holy wisdom and mildness the present, exceedingly wretched condition of their co-religionists. May you deign to cast a gracious glance from your exalted throne upon those, who, though Israelites, are a portion of your people.

Your Holiness gave them permission to occupy houses for dwelling and business purposes beyond the boundaries set in earlier times. They have gradually perceived that this concession has not produced the beneficial effects which, without doubt, lay in the thought of your Holiness. The streets which by that concession they could use are very narrow. Room for residence purposes has been further diminished by the palaces and religious institutions here and there, so that many families that otherwise would have removed from the old section remained there. Therefore the contiguity of the houses and the massing of the inhabitants, with all the resultant evils, continue much as they were twenty-two years ago.

These evils are most noticeable in Azinelle, Catalana and Fiumara streets.

These, inhabited for the most part by the poorest classes, chiefly rag-pickers and sellers of old soles, defy all the laws of health.

In the streets Azinelle and Catalana, light and air are very scarce. Seldom or never does a ray of the sun penetrate there; yet small, narrow ground-floors must serve for dwellings and stores. This condition of affairs brings forth even worse results in Fiumara street, which lies so low that whenever the Tiber rises floods ensue, and the dampness which remains long after the water has receded becomes a source of disease, jeopardizing health and often life. The prohibition to have stores outside of the set boundaries, considered from another point of view, is no less injurious to the Israelites. They meet with difficulties, sometimes insuperable, if they desire to devote their activity to some occupation besides trading, more particularly trading in clothes. They cast their eye upon many branches of industry, art and science; but in the condition to which they have been degraded, they can entertain no hope of entering upon any other career.

In the retail and wholesale branches of the clothing business, which formerly they controlled, foreign and home competitors have arisen in the past few decades. These competitors, with their magnificent stores situated in the most populous and the richest portions of the city, have drawn greatly from the trade of the Israelites, confined, as they are, to a single and less prominent section. As a result, many have been entirely ruined; others have continued to eke out a living with care and trouble; still others, the richest men of the community, discouraged by their losses, deprived of the right to own real estate, which would have secured their fortune, have emigrated to other lands, leaving the great majority to whom they had given help and imparted advice. These now of necessity sink to even lower depths of wretchedness.

It certainly does not escape your wise insight, Holy Father, how such a concurrence of difficulties must greatly increase the burdens of the pious Israelitish institutions, which were founded, and are almost entirely supported by private charity. For, owing to the above mentioned emigration of those families who formerly managed the different institutions, and endeavored, with great zeal and love, to improve them, only sparse and occasional revenues remain to meet the greatest and most pressing needs. The difficulties of providing for their own support, prevent those to whom the management of these institutions has now fallen from devoting themselves to the work, all the more necessary since destitution is continually increasing. This community has not sufficient means to alleviate the want, for its status as fixed by law and its poverty prevent any attempt towards that end from being successful.

The Jewish community has, it is true, founded an elementary school for religious and civic instruction, but impelled by hunger, the son of poor parents leaves school while of tender years in order to procure the piece of bread with which his parents cannot supply him, and to look for a rag with which to cover his nakedness. Pack-carrier, rag-picker, vender of matches, messenger and waiter, buyer of old soles, water carrier, bearer of burdens, he becomes, and never, never anything else ! No other nourishment for his intellectual and moral nature ! His forehead— persecutions have pressed the seal of contempt on it—cannot boast of the noble sweat of work, his hand cannot show the honorable hardness of the workman's. Abandoned to his poverty, deprived of all means to combat it energetically, he eventually comes to identify himself completely with his misery. He cannot even hope for an alleviation of his condition such as others can find in the tasks which the municipality provides. He instinctively feels that he has been robbed of the most precious possessions here below, and in his despair he loses all consciousness of his human dignity. He celebrates weddings which have no joy for him ; even the family loses its exalted character. In the dismal room, exposed to all the influences of bitter poverty, a single bed stands, upon which, regardless of every consideration of

health and chastity, parents and the troop
of children of every age and sex lie down
together. The governing body of the
community, indeed, takes account of the
moral disorder and the diseases which such
a state of affairs causes ; but how can any
preventive measures be effectually adopted
when there are hundreds and hundreds of
such families ! And although you, Holy
Father, took this community, too, under
the wings of your exalted kindness, and gave
it a share of the state charities, yet did
those unto whom the carrying out of the
merciful act of the great sovereign was intrusted, devote but three hundred scudi to
this purpose, notwithstanding the fact that
more than two thousand poor are enrolled
for weekly alms. Those of moderate means
exhaust their resources in the struggle
with the burdens which they are compelled
to bear, viz., the taxes which they have to
pay in common with the whole population,
and the special tax imposed on their religious community. They are also obliged,
besides paying other taxes of the congregation, to give a fixed sum yearly to two

Catholic foundations, the *casa pia* of the catechumens and the convent of the converts, two institutions for the conversion of Jews, and must pay the expenses of the governing body of the Jewish community, which consists of non-Jews. With each biennial renewal of the so-called tax for industry and capital, they complain of the continual increase of the sums they must expend in consequence of the falling off of other contributions due to business misfortunes, and they accuse the administration of arbitrariness and injustice."

The memorial then goes on to give at length a history of the Jewish community of Rome, dwelling upon the kindness of the popes towards the Jews and their favorable position up to the time of Paul IV. The later legislation, which, in spite of occasional intervals of clemency, gradually depressed and degraded the Jews, is set forth in detail. "The unfortunates, oppressed in the present, despairing of the future, excluded from civil rights, grew less and less familiar to the community at large, and at the same time more and

more powerless to fight the slanders directed against their domestic and communal life, their religious belief and their
history, so that their spiritual . elasticity
was lamed, and their naturally great en-
ergy weakened. Thus they sank in the
estimation of their fellow citizens, and .
what was still more deplorable, in that of
the exalted popes by whom they had been
so highly honored formerly."

The petition adduces evidence from
non-Jewish sources of the worth of many
of the Jews of Rome, speaks of the remarkable careers of Jewish physicians
who attended popes, cardinals and other
dignitaries, calls attention to the learned
Jews of Rome, such as Nathan ben Jechiel,
compiler of the *Aruch*, the first Talmudical dictionary, Immanuel, the poet, the
friend of Dante, Giulio Romano, the philosopher, and others, and closes with the
following strong prayer :

"Accustomed as the undersigned are to
bless your name, they hope not to have
spoken in vain to your fatherly heart of
the sad lot still theirs ; the insalubrity of

the old Jewish dwellings ; the exceedingly
contracted space granted the Jews for
homes ; the direct and indirect obstacles
to the free pursuit of the trades, the fine
arts and the larger number of industries ;
the limited right to possess real estate ;
the denial on the part of some notaries of
their right to act as witnesses; the alarm-
ing increase of poverty; the impotence of
the Israelitish benevolent institutions to
prevent or lessen misery ; the impropriety
of the yearly appropriations paid by order
of the finance commission to two Catholic
institutions; the alarm of the rich, who, in
consequence of the mentioned burdens,
are subjected to many pecuniary sacri-
fices required by their own religious
foundations, and others which the indebt-
edness of their benevolent institutions
demands of them ; the inability to take
energetic measures for the better educa-
tion of the greatly increasing poorer class—
all this (misery), O Holy Father, must
appeal to you, in such a degree, that your
own heart will find it advisable not to delay
the carrying out of the good deed, for

pauperes facti sumus nimis, we have become too impoverished, and the prayer
which the undersigned whisper in the
hearing of your Holiness is the prayer of
forty-eight hundred of your subjects.

Hear us, O Holy Father, so that the
children of Israel may once again benefit
by that noble generosity inseparably connected with your immortal name !"

The day of deliverance, however, was
at hand, arriving sooner than they had
expected. While the Jews of Rome were
preparing this petition for the final abolition of the Ghetto, the pope was still master of the destinies of the city. But the
occasion never came to present it, for the
temporal sway of the pope came to an end,
when on September 20, 1870, the Italian
kingdom with Victor Immanuel as king
was established. The Jews changed masters. They welcomed their king enthusiastically. New hopes were aroused in the
Jewish community. The Ghettos established by the popes were virtually abolished.
The Ghetto of Rome stood, it is true, fifteen years longer. It was only in 1885

that it began to be demolished, having stood longer than any Ghetto in western Europe. But now this remnant of mediæval exclusion has passed away. The Jews of Rome, with new opportunities, are taking an honored position among their Italian countrymen. It is a long story of oppression, lasting just eighteen hundred years, from the destruction of the Temple of Jerusalem and the deportation of the Jewish captives to Rome in 70, to the accession of Victor Immanuel in 1870. Eighteen hundred years! Rome has had many masters. Emperors, northern conquerors, popes, Rienzi, powerful families, such as the Colonnas, Orsinis, Borgias, have appeared on the scene, and lived their short day. Through it all, in that wretched quarter on the Tiber, amid disadvantages inconceivable and under burdens vast, the Jewish community lived on, unchanged amid change, steadfast in oppression, firm in faith and trust in the God of their fathers! The tocsin of freedom has sounded, and from out the dark hole of forced seclusion Judaism's

followers have issued into the broad light
of liberty. Let others account for it as
they may ; we see, in the long history and
the continued existence of this people, the
hand of Providence directing the course
of those who lived and suffered for the
truth.

May prosperity find the descendants of
the Jews of the Ghetto as faithful as ad-
versity found their ancestors !

CHAPTER VII.

THE RUSSIAN GHETTO.

The *Judengasse* of Frankfort has become a memory, the *Judenstadt* of Prague has ceased to be the compulsory dwelling place of the Jews, the Ghetto of Rome has been demolished—everywhere in Europe relics of hostile legislation have disappeared before the enlightened, tolerant spirit of the age. Everywhere? Nay, not so. We should have said, everywhere west of the boundaries of the empire of the Tzar. There, in barbarous Russia, the mediæval spirit still rules, and a Ghetto exists whose condition is more horrible perhaps than ever that of any Ghetto of earlier days. It stands forth in a blackness the more intense because of the sun of tolerance that shines everywhere else. It is not the Ghetto with which we have become acquainted thus far, a street or section set apart in a town or city, but a district set

12 (177)

apart in a country. The Jew is told, "only
in certain sections of the land you may
dwell." The Russian persecutions are
the crime of the century, and this massing
of millions of people within a comparatively small section, and closing the whole
of the remaining portion of the land against
them is the height of malicious ingenuity.
This Russian Ghetto is known as the
Pale of Settlement. In the whole of Russia, not counting Poland (for "in stealing
Poland, Russia had to take its Jews, too"),
Jews are permitted to reside only in the
following fifteen *gubernia :* Wilna, Kowno,
Vitebsk, Grodno, Minsk, Moghilev, Vol-
hynia, Podolia, in West Russia ; Kiev
(exclusive of the city of Kiev), Tchernigov and Poltava, in the Ukraine or Little
Russia ; Ekaterinoslav, Taurida (except
Sebastopol), Kherson (except Nikolaiev),
and Bessarabia, in South Russia. From
Great Russia, from the provinces of Kazan
and Astrakhan, from Finland and the Bal-
tic Provinces they are entirely excluded.[122]
Even in the Pale of Settlement they are
permitted to dwell in the cities only, and

thus there has been created a Pale within the Pale. What makes the crowding within these pens the harder to bear is the fact that for a time a little light had appeared, and the Jews had been permitted under certain conditions to dwell outside the Pale of Settlement. Alexander II had lightened the burden of the Jews somewhat, and in 1865 had granted permission to dwell where they pleased to Jews in possession of university diplomas, to merchants of the first guild, and to artisans. Besides, Jews were tolerated in the principal ports, such as Riga, Libau, Rostov. The number who had taken advantage of this permission reached hundreds of thousands. After the assassination of the humane Tzar, the evil days began. A spirit of fanaticism, fed by cries of pan-slavism and supremacy of the Russian orthodox religion, became rampant, and the first victims to feel the terrible effects were the Jews. In May, 1882, by the inspiration of the tyrant Ignatieff, the so-called May laws, fraught with so much misery, were promulgated. These laws

ordered (1) that as a temporary measure,
until a general revision of the laws concerning the Jews can be made in a proper
manner, the Jews be forbidden to settle
outside the towns, the only exceptions being in Jewish colonies that existed before,
and whose inhabitants are agriculturists;
and (2) that the completion of instru-
ments of purchase of real property and
mortgages in the name of Jews, the regis-
tration of Jews as lessees of landed estates
situated outside the precincts of towns,
and the issue of powers of attorney to
enable Jews to manage and dispose of
such property, be suspended temporarily.[123]
These laws were made to refer to the Pale
of Settlement. The Russo-Jewish Committee of London commenting on these
laws says, " The effect of the first clause of
this enactment would clearly be to create
a Pale within the Pale. Hitherto, ordinary Jews, if prevented from going beyond the Pale, could move from town to
village, and from village to village, within
the Pale. This was to be stopped. In
process of time, all the Jews of the Pale

would be cooped up in the towns and townlets found within it. There they might be left 'to stew in their own juice.'

The second clause was not wide-reaching in its scope, for it tended to the same end, by restricting still further the possibility of Jewish life in the country. If a Jew might not acquire land by pur-chase, mortgage or lease, or have any-thing to do with landed estate, his country life must come to an end, and even the favored exceptions, permitted to reside in the villages as old inhabitants, would have no work to occupy them."[124] Upon the enforcement of these laws, the popula-tions of the overcrowded cities and towns were augmented by the thousands com-pelled to leave their homes in the country and the villages ; it amounted to virtual expulsion, for, unable to find a resting place, the unfortunates had to leave Rus-sia. The expulsions of 1882 are still fresh in the minds of all. The unprece-dented cruelty and inhumanity of these May laws called forth so indignant a pro-test in Western Europe and in America

as to bring about the deposal of Ignatieff
from favor, and with it the partial suspen-
sion of his laws. But the persecuting
spirit has been at work, and since 1888,
when it broke forth more strongly than
ever, the May laws have been rigorously
enforced. A new power had arisen in
the land. Pobiedonostseff, the primate
of the Russian church, a man possessed
of that "true malignity of genius that
makes a grand inquisitor," had obtained
complete mastery over the Tzar's mind.
The miseries of the Russian Jews have
increased hundredfold. The crowding
into the cities of the Pale goes on apace.
Towns such as Tchernigov, of five thousand Jews, have had the number increased
to twenty thousand.

So Berditchev in the province of Kiev,
in 1890, was supposed to contain about
60,000 inhabitants, two-thirds Jews. An
acute observer says of the effects of the
edicts upon this town : "It was then an
overcrowded place, made up for the most
part of old and insanitary rookeries, in
which was huddled one of the poorest

populations to be found anywhere in Europe. By August, 1891, it was said that fully twenty thousand additional Hebrews had been driven in from the surrounding country. The spectacle of their poverty and squalor was something too sickening for words. The whole place, with its filthy streets, its reeking half-cellars under the overhanging balconies, and its swarming throngs of unwashed, unkempt wretches, packed into the narrow thoroughfares on the lookout for food, made a picture scarcely human. Mr. Pennell tells me that when he was there in November he was assured that, instead of the sixty thousand Jews of August, there were then in Berditchev no less than ninety thousand * * * There are over a hundred towns in that hell called the Pale where the same causes operate which have made Berditchev such an unspeakable charnel-house, and in each one the Russian police have done their brutal best to reproduce the conditions of Berditchev."[125]

What are the poor creatures to do? Harried and harassed, they are veritable

pariahs and outcasts. The Jews in the
cities and towns of the Pale are poor
enough, and to have the number trebled
and quadrupled means lack of sustenance
for all. Even the privileged classes, those
permitted to dwell without the Pale, are
rapidly decreasing. How soon, by confiscation and systematic robbery on the part
of the officials, may not a merchant of the
first guild sink into the second? Then off
into the Pale, no matter now long he may
have dwelt in his home! Artisans, too,
had been granted permission to dwell anywhere. But what constitutes an artisan?
The authorities decide. For instance, in
one province it was decided that Jewish
bakers, butchers, etc., are not artisans, and
they have been driven out. The word is
very elastic, particularly since the law limits
it by the adjective "skilled,"[126] and so the
authorities (for in Russia every official, no
matter how low or how high his rank,
considers himself an authority) interpret
the term as they please, and the Jews are
completely at the mercy of every official,
from the ordinary policeman up to the

governor of the province. Jews with
university diplomas are among the privileged classes, permitted to reside anywhere, but the government has taken care
to limit those entitled to enjoy choice of
residence, by passing laws providing that
only a very small percentage of students
may be Jews.[127] Restrictions everywhere!
Prohibitions on all sides! Gradually and
surely the Jews are forced into the cities
of the Pale. The Russian Ghetto! oh,
the misery, the horror of it all! Stories
innumerable of cruelty almost incredible
have come to us—of soldiers who had
served in the army for years coming back to
their native place, being treated as strangers, and driven out;[128] of artisans, resi-
dents of villages all their lives, going for
a week or a month to some other place
for work, and on their return being treated
as newcomers, their former residence ig-
nored; of Jewish girls, who, to remain
with their parents, had themselves enrolled
as prostitutes (this class of women being
permitted to dwell anywhere in Russia),
and because they would not ply the

nefarious trade, were driven out. And
then the terrible results in the cities of the
Pale! The crowding of thousands of
homeless, suffering, destitute Jews into
the already swarming, dirty, ill-built, half-
starving towns, deepened the prevailing
misery. Sickness and disease ran riot.
Phthisis, which had been practically unknown among Jews, led to the rejection
of 6.5 per cent of Jewish recruits as
against 0 5 per cent of other Russians.
Other maladies hitherto unknown arose
among them.[12] Another source of misery
was the re-enforcement of an old law
permitted to fall into neglect. This
law, first suggested in 1816,[13] had ordered
that no Jew should dwell within fifty versts
(thirty-three miles) of the frontier. It
became a dead letter. Hundreds of thousands of Jews settled within this district.
The old law has been revived, and is being
enforced. So the people who have dwelt
for years within the forbidden limits are
likewise forced back into the Pale.

Things have been growing worse all the
time; in 1891 they reached their climax;

new edicts of expulsion of even the privileged classes, permitted to dwell in the
cities, were promulgated—edicts upon
edicts. For example, in Moscow, on July
28th, appeared regulations in regard to the
artisans, who were divided into three
classes : (1) those living in Moscow only
three years, unmarried or childless, and
employing only one workman ; (2) those
of six years residence, with four children and
four workmen ; (3) those having "a very
long residence" and a "large family," and
more than four workmen. For these expulsion was decreed, for the first class,
within from three to six months ; for the
second, within from six to nine months ;
for the third, within from nine to twelve
months. To this was attached a rider to
the effect that (*a*) all clerks, personal attend-
ants and those of small occupations must
go within six months ; (*b*) all engaged in
trade, especially in large factories owned
by Russians, must go within one year.[13]
This in Moscow ; St. Petersburg, " holy "
Kiev, even Odessa, although within the Pale,
have like stories to tell. The Jews must go.

By law or by arbitrary decree, Russia outside the Pale must be cleansed of them, and
it is being gradually done. Imagination
cannot picture the unfeeling cruelty of it all.
Hundreds of thousands of innocent, unof-
fending citizens deprived of their homes
and possessions, and forced into new,
strange dwelling places, unable to support
their own teeming populations! It means
nothing short of expulsion or death. The
number of Jews dwelling within the Russian Ghetto, or Pale, in 1884, was esti-
mated at 2,920,639. A rough calculation
has been made of the Jews who by the
new edicts and restrictions have been and
will be expelled from their homes and
forced into the cities of the Pale :[132]

Expulsion from villages inside the Pale is estimated to affect	500,000
Expulsion of artisans outside the Pale,	200,000
Expulsion from commercial towns outside the Pale,	500,000
Expulsion from the fifty-verst zone. . .	250,000
	1,450,000

Add these to the swarming populations
residing in the cities of the Pale, and it
will be readily understood that never has

there been, even in the darkest days, a
Ghetto with accompanying circumstances
more dreadful than this, existing in sight of
the enlightened world of the year eighteen
hundred and ninety-four of Christian civilization. The Middle Ages, with all their
fanaticism and intolerance, have nothing
to show surpassing it in systematic
cruelty. Mediæval church laws at least
pretend to give a reason for separating
the dwelling places of Jews from those of
Christians; it was feared that the latter
would be contaminated by contact with
the former. In the autocracy of Eastern
Europe there is not even the pretense of
a reason or excuse. The laws are made;
it is the tyrant's will—that is the end of
the matter. Possibly the same idea holds,
that holy Russia may be contaminated by
the presence of Jews. Considering the
Jews a pest, the Russian rulers enclose
them in the Ghetto as in a lazaretto.

"These laws regulating the dwelling
place of the Jews present the most shock-
ing anomalies. They put the Jews below
the criminals to whom certain cities, nota-

bly the capitals, are forbidden only for a
specified period after the expiration of their
sentence.   *   *   *   *   According to the
letter of the law, the greatest sculptor of
Russia, Antokolsky, correspondent of our
Institute, has not the right to live in St.
Petersburg.

Do the Jews enjoy the same rights as
the other subjects of the Tzar, at least in
the mentioned district (the Pale), in which
they are confined? By no means. They
are deprived of several all-important
rights. They are forbidden to acquire
land in the provinces in which they are
forced to live. They are forbidden even
to lease land outside of the cities. They
cannot be farmers."[133]

It is the same old story over again:
Jews forced into the cities, forbidden to
own land, and then reproached for not
being farmers. For eighteen hundred
years the present Russian policy was the
policy of all European states; the Jews
could not be farmers had they wanted to.
The Jews of Russia are to-day in the
same situation as the Jews of Europe gen-

erally before the close of the last century.
They know not where to lay their head.
Certainly, the prospect of emigration is
theirs, but the emigration is forced ; they
are literally driven out, for to go into the
Ghetto set apart for them is well-nigh
synonymous with stepping into a death
trap ; disease, hunger, starvation await
them there. Rich men beggared in a
month, honorable men chased from their
homes like criminals, ambitious students
driven from the universities to go they
know not whither, unless to the Ghetto or
to strange lands—these are the sad experiences that hundreds and thousands of Russian Jews have lived through in the past
ten years. And within that Pale of Settlement, what a terrifying future presents itself ! Five, eight, ten persons struggling
for a livelihood where one can scarcely
find sufficient sustenance. Degeneracy,
physical, mental, moral. Millions subjected to the very worst conditions of life.
Bad enough before the enforcement of the
May laws, infinitely worse now; the overcrowded towns are breeders of disease

and contagion. The evils and horrors of the Ghetto have re-appeared in
their worst form. The future is all
dark, not one streak of light to relieve
the gloom—no hope of improvement!
The miserable, embittered existence of
these poor creatures has no prospect of
betterment. Death alone will make them
free. It is like an oppressive nightmare.
But retribution will come. Into Darkest
Russia, too, the light must penetrate.
" He sleeps not, neither does He slumber,
the guardian of Israel." The Russian
Ghetto will be swept from the face of the
earth, as in their time all Ghettos have disappeared. The wide expanse of the
Russian empire, too, will be opened to the
Jew, and the frightful conditions of to-day
will pass away. Right is might, and with
such a champion, the poor, harried, persecuted Russian Jew will conquer, though
all the powers of darkness be arrayed in
the lists against him to-day. The abolition of the Ghetto, the Pale of Settlement, the full right of the Jew to live and
settle in Russia where it pleases him, is

the only solution of the Russo-Jewish
problem. [134]

CHAPTER VIII.

EFFECTS AND RESULTS.

The enforced seclusion of a people during centuries, as told in the foregoing chapters, cannot but produce characteristic results. That Jews in many places and instances, still show the effects of the Ghetto period, cannot be doubted. It is not yet half a century since they have gained full political and social emancipation in Western Europe. The habits formed during centuries cannot be expected to wear off in a few decades. The unpleasant traits of the Jews are due to the persecutions ; their virtues are the resultant of the strong hold of their religion upon them.

Who will wonder at the evil effects which exclusion had on the development of the Jew, physically and mentally ? Pen up a mass of people for centuries in narrow, unhealthy streets and noisome quar-

ters, and what results may be expected ?
Owing to the unhealthiness of the Jew's
environment, he could not develop physically, and thus became stunted in body.
Owing to his enforced occupations, small
peddling and money transactions, he gradually in his relations to the outer world, became a fearful, terrified, stricken creature,
and these things naturally reacted on the
mind. Shut off from all contact with the
world at large, the Jew within the walls of
the Ghetto naturally did not respond to
the culture of the world. Learning, certainly, there always was, and learning was
held in the highest respect ; but it was
the learning of the ancients, the Talmud
and rabbinical dialectics. These studies
sharpened the mind, it is true, and later,
when emancipation came, the Jewish in-
tellect, exercised for centuries in this
dialectical training school, readily mas-
tered the difficulties of the various
branches of learning in the universities.
But in the Ghetto, notably in Germany
and the countries of Eastern Europe,
this terrible, systematic exclusion of the

Jews from all contact with the outer world contracted the mind, and prevented all cultivation of learning outside of Jewish studies.

The wonder is that in spite of the mountain-load of disadvantages, disabilities, and wrongs, the Jew preserved himself as well as he did. For evil as were the effects, physical and mental, little as the Jews produced of works of general literature, philosophy, and science between the fifteenth and the eighteenth centuries, yet the moral side of Jewish life, as reflected in the beauty of the home, in the charity, purity, and chastity of the community and of the individual, even the systematic caging in the Ghetto by church and state did not affect for the worse. This moral purity was not sullied, and in spite of all the disadvantages of situation, the virtues that crown the life of man with man here found constant cultivation and application. The Ghetto possibly brought these things out in stronger relief. Family ties were strengthened, domestic purity shone the brighter, because only in the home and in the family the Jew was a free man. The

hand of power that rested with such crushing weight upon him without could not
penetrate within. Here he was king.
The glory of his ancestors, the pride
of race, possessed him. God was with
him, of that he was sure ; his troubles
would come to an end at some time. This
light not all the waves of oppression could
extinguish. In the Ghetto, too, it shone.
Herein lay the salvation of the Jew. His
inner life appeared all the more brilliant
when contrasted with the darkness of his
external position. The Jew saved himself
by force of those virtues which will redeem
man from any condition, even though it
be as untoward and foreboding as the
prison-like confinement of the Jews for
centuries within the walls and gates. of the
Ghetto.

The Ghetto gave rise to social habits
and customs peculiar to its inhabitants.
Shut off, as they were, from communication
with the remainder of the community,
thrown entirely upon their own resources,
and associating only with each other, they
developed among themselves that peculiar

Ghetto life, which, in our day, has received
such masterly portrayal at the hands of
Kompert, Bernstein, Franzos, Kohn, and
others, to whom I shall have occasion to
refer again.   Perhaps the most striking
product of the Ghetto was the language
there spoken.   In early days, the language
which Jews spoke differed in nowise
from that of their neighbors, but in time
there was formed the peculiar speech
of the Ghetto, the *Jüdisch-deutsch*, a jargon.   This language was a mixture of
Hebrew and German terms in various
peculiar combinations, with a liberal sprink-
ling of words of other European languages,
as *e. g., blett*, a ticket entitling the holder
to a meal, the French *billet; benshen*, to
bless, the Latin *benedire : frimselich*, a kind
of pastry, the Italian *vermicelli ;* all showing traces of the days when the Jews spoke
these languages.   A treatise on this
strange linguistic development remains
to be written,[135] although some good work
has been done by several scholars, the
beginning having been made by *Alt-
meister* Zunz, who in his epoch-making

work, *Die gottesdienstlichen Vorträge der Juden*, devotes several pages[136] to a discussion of the "jargon," and gives the rules that seem to have been employed in the formation of terms, as well as a list of words and phrases. The "jargon" is a product of the past ; with the fall of the walls of the Ghetto, it disappeared, like so many of the alleged peculiarities to which the oppression of centuries gave rise among Jews.

But certain effects of Ghetto existence upon the Jew are apparent even to-day. A recent writer has well said: " People who have been living in a Ghetto for a couple of centuries are not able to step outside merely because the gates are thrown down, nor to efface the brands on their souls by putting off the yellow badges. The isolation from without will have come to seem the law of their being."[137] Even in this free country of ours, where a Ghetto has never been established by religious canon or civil law, the effects of Ghetto life in Europe crop out very perceptibly. In our larger cities, Jewish quarters are being formed,

which, though not defined by law, nor enclosed by walls, nor barred by gates, to all
intents and purposes are no less Ghettos
than those of mediæval days. The poorer
Jews who come to this country naturally
flock together, and inhabit whole districts
which come to assume the appearance of
Ghettos. So it is also in London, Amsterdam, Paris, Vienna, and other large cities of
Europe. The Ghetto in law has ceased to
be; the Ghetto in fact still exists. Now,
this *esprit de corps*, this exclusiveness, this
seeking of brethren, is a direct result of
the treatment to which Jews have been
subjected during the Christian centuries.
And not alone the masses of poor, wretched
creatures that live in the lowly quarters of the great cities of the world, but
even those Jews who have reaped all the
benefits of emancipation, and move in the
higher circles of life and thought, are often
met with the reproach that they are clannish and exclusive, that they shut themselves up within their own social precincts,
and are attracted to one another by a
magnetism of fellowship. Very true, and

very natural; so long were the Jews excluded by legal measure and enactment
and religious prejudice and teaching from
all intimate contact with non-Jews, so long
were they thrown upon one another, that as
a logical result, they became exclusive.
People maltreated and oppressed for the
same reason cling to one another. Suffering in a like cause attaches them very close
to each other, for there is no bond that
unites so firmly as suffering. The Jew
was excluded, therefore he became exclusive; he was avoided, therefore he became clannish; the hand of the world was
against him, therefore he sought protection
amongst his own. Even though official exclusion be a thing of the past, the
prejudices of men and churches cannot be
abolished by law and decree, and largely
· these still exist against the Jew. He has
met his fellow-man more than half way.
The most liberal expressions emanate
from the Jewish pulpit and the pens of
Jewish authors,[138] but rarely are they recip-
rocated. The great consensus of opinion
in the Christian world still considers the

Jew as lost, and, as though he were heathen, fit subject for missionary effort. As long as this is the state of the case, expressed or implied, the Jews are forced in upon themselves. As long as this arrogant assumption of superiority marks the attitude of Christianity, so long can there be no meeting on common ground. Equality pre-supposes mutual respect, and the attitude of the churches that consider the Jew damned for all eternity, unless he be baptized in the name of the Christian Saviour, although not expressed in words, is the same as that of the mediæval church, which ever spoke and wrote of Judaism as superstition and perfidy. Advances cannot all come from one side. If the ill effects of bygone centuries are ever to be entirely overcome, the Christian world must concede full and equal liberty to Jews to think and believe as they will, leaving the final judgment unto Him who looks into the hearts of men.

Another time-honored accusation continually flung at Jews is, that they are merely consumers, and not producers; that

they are to be found in commercial pursuits only, and not in the handicrafts; that
they flock to the cities and monopolize
trade, and are rarely, if ever, found tilling
the soil. Superficial observation seems
to confirm these statements, but it must
be emphatically stated that the Jews themselves are not to blame; that this is one
of the effects of Ghetto life, Ghetto
legislation, and Christian treatment of
Jews. More than a century ago, Moses
Mendelssohn, in response to the same
reproach, pithily said: "Our hands are
bound, and we are blamed for not using
them." If the Jews were not conspicuous
in trades and industrial branches at the
time when these were honorable pursuits,
it was not their fault, but that of the governments under which they lived. The
limits of the guilds were so narrow and
circumscribed, they were governed by
such exclusive laws, that no Jew, before
the time of general emancipation, could
break through the barriers. When the
note of freedom and emancipation
sounded, and the governments began to

grant the Jews rights as citizens, and passed decrees favorable to their entering the trades, then the Jews themselves put forth efforts in this direction.

In biblical times the Jews were an agricultural, not a commercial people. The many notices, too, in the Talmud and other Jewish writings on the honorable character of trades, and the necessity of engaging in them, at once dispel the notion that the Jews were opposed to these pursuits. We need only refer to learned men specially mentioned as having gained their livelihood by the trades of the collier, shoemaker, carpenter, smith. But when the Jews were scattered over Europe's wide domain, all changed from what it had been in Palestine and Babylonia. They lived now under Christian governments, which, in conjunction with the priesthood, did all in their power, if not to exterminate, for that was impossible, at least, to hamper and degrade the Jews. They were compelled to resort to those means by which they could gain some hold of power. This their money gave them. Hence their pre-

eminence in commerce and in money transactions. They cultivated these activities.
Gold and silver satisfied the rapacity of
their oppressors, and gained them respite
from suffering. All the energies of the
acute Jewish mind being turned to commerce, they brought it to a high state of
perfection, invented bills of exchange,
became the bankers and the merchants
of mediæval Europe. There was ample
reason, then, for their not engaging in the
trades. Self-preservation forced them
into commercial life. It must also be
remembered that there was a period
when the trades and handicrafts were
in the hands of the lowest classes, being
pursued by either slaves, or women, or by
the free classes ineligible to a military
career. It is, therefore, not surprising
that Jews, severely oppressed because
of their religion, did not wish to debase
themselves further by engaging in occupations in themselves considered degrading.

When the trades rose in general estimation, we find Jews mentioned here and

there as farmers, as growers of the vine, as mechanics. But gradually these trades and industries enclosed themselves within narrow confines, and against attempts of governments to open the trades to Jews, it was urged that if they were admitted, their competition would soon work to the detriment of Christian workmen. Always the same clamor : the Jews place others at a disadvantage, therefore, they must be kept down and out, and, if this be possible by no other means, force must be employed. Perhaps this has never been better stated than by Gabriel Riesser, the redoubtable champion of Jewish emancipation : "Commerce requires many and distant—trades, few and close, connections. As long as the hatred of the Christian prevented a close relation to Jews, they could be associated in commerce, but not in the trades. This circumstance sufficiently explains, without Sabbath or Talmud, why Jews, until the last century, could engage so little in handicrafts."

It was the oft repeated cry : contact with the accursed Jews may lead to terrible consequences. Out with them! out with them! cried the workman. The greater the number of competitors, the more difficult for each to gain his livelihood. Lower, lower press them down, away from all association with their fellows of other faiths! Every honorable occupation was closed to them. The power of the trade guilds was great, they resented all attempts of governments to interfere in their affairs. Whithersoever the Jew turned, he was conscious of lofty though invisible walls. Each century but added to the burden of the preceding century. The load was becoming heavier and heavier. Oft in anguish of soul the Jews cried aloud, for it seemed impossible to bear with such indignities any longer. Money transactions, or worse, peddling and hawking, were the only avenues open for earning a livelihood. The *Schacherjude* was a creature evolved by circumstances and the systematic course resorted to by his enemies to degrade the Jew. The only countries wherein Jews could and did engage in the trades were those in which they dwelt in sufficiently large numbers (as the different provinces of Poland), so that there was no need of others to assist them and associate with them.

But the time of reckoning was coming. The recording angel had almost done with the tale of governmental exclusion and persecution of Jews. The measure was full. The time was ripe. Mankind was awakening from the stupor of ages. Humanity was to assert its rights. The eighteenth century stands as the dividing line between the old and the new. Aye, the eighteenth century! Blessed time, when humanity spoke, and advocated the claims of all the children of men; when the false and rank growths of mediævalism fell before the purifying influence of awakened reason, even like a crumbling ruin swept by the storm. The American Revolution "fired the shot heard round the world," and the old, corrupt society of Europe was shaken

to its depths by the reverberation.
France, all combustible, needed but the
spark ; it fell, and the French Revolution,
an explosion of the magazines wherein
had accumulated the rubbish of centuries,
moved Europe from end to end. The
new time was inaugurated. Mankind was
freed. Humanity ruled. Governments
listened. The abuses of ages were laid bare.
Unto the Jew, also, the most wronged
of Europe's inhabitants, the new era
brought its glad tidings. Kings and rulers
turned their attention to the improvement of the lot of their Jewish subjects.
The avenues which had been closed to them
were gradually opened. Within sixty years
after the beginning of the nineteenth century, the Jew was a free man in Western
Europe. France, leader in humane
acts and liberal thoughts, was followed
by German princes, by Italy, by England. The walls of the Ghetto had
fallen ; the world was open to the Jew,
and among the earliest privileges was
the right to engage in trades and industries. It is remarkable with what

14

eagerness this permission was seized. Undoubtedly their leaders felt that it was necessary to remove the byword of peddler,
money-lender, from the Jews, and to make
them more readily affiliate with their Christian neighbors. Societies were started in
the early decades of this century for the
purpose of furthering trades among the
Jews in Prussia, Frankfort, Bavaria, Baden,
Saxony, Pomerania, Hessen, Hamburg,
the Saxon duchies. Jewish boys were
apprenticed. Industrial schools were instituted. Ere long there were Jewish
master mechanics all through Germany.
They followed trades of every kind and
description. They became shoemakers,
tailors, saddlers, bookbinders, locksmiths,
bakers, weavers, printers, cutlers, watch-
makers, furriers, lithographers, and the
like. Land, too, was beginning to be
bought, and here and there Jewish farmers
were heard of. Factories were started by
Jews, who employed workmen of all
classes, both of their own faith and others.
They assisted the governments wherever
the slightest hope was given that their dis-

abilities would be removed. The Jews themselves entered upon the work with a will, and it is most encouraging to reflect upon their early efforts to improve the new opportunities granted by the governments. The inner development was such that within seventy years after Mendelssohn's death, his co-religionists enjoyed all the rights of men and citizens in the land where he, one of the most distinguished of philosophers and scholars, was regarded as an alien.

In 1848 most of the disabilities resting upon Jews were removed in the countries of western Europe. How has it been since, there and in America? We still hear of the enormous wealth of the Jews. We are told that if one walks down Broadway in New York, the great majority of the firms are Jewish. The Jewish commercial spirit still forms the refrain of many a prejudice. Whenever anti-Semitism has raised its head in late years, this has been one of its cries. The Jew lives off of the poor Christian workman. The Christian must toil; the Jew enjoys. The Christian is poor; the Jew is rich. The Jew works not with his hands at honest toil; he cannot be found in the factories, he cannot be found in the fields, farming and gardening; only in the street, buying and selling. Such invidious distinctions are still drawn, although careful observation must prove that there is no truth in them. The ideas of mediævalism have not been banished from the popular mind. The Jew is still looked upon as standing apart. The conception has not yet gained ground that the only distinction is one of religion. This truth the Jews must emphasize in word and in work. And in no better way can it be emphasized and fully proved than by his standing at the same forge, or sitting on the same bench with others. Trades and industries will bring close connections.

It is now felt that one solution of the problem thrust upon the Jews of Western Europe and America by the immigration of hordes of Russian exiles is to form them into agricultural communities. This will require time, money and patience.

The Russian Jews are issuing from a condition like unto that in which the Jews generally found themselves throughout Europe in the Ghetto period. They, too, must become accustomed to their new life. What they are is owing not to themselves, but to their government. The taste for new occupations must be fostered ; many a drawback and obstacle will be encountered, but perseverance and time will gain the victory. The Jews must be their own redeemers, and they alone can and will overcome the effect of the exclusiveness of the Ghetto period, which, by closing every other occupation to them, forced them into the lines of money-changing, peddling, and hawking. The injustice of popular condemnation has never stood forth so clearly as in this instance of reproaching the Jews for that wherein they fail, their failure being due not to their own shortcomings, but to the treatment, or rather maltreatment, which they have received.

The remarkable progress made by individual Jews in the universities of Europe

and in the learned professions, as soon as
these were thrown open to them, has often
been the subject of remark and surprise,
and speeches and writings of anti-Semites
are full of warnings to the effect that Jews,
enjoying even now more than their due
proportion of professorial chairs, and
journalistic and professional honors, will
eventually monopolize them. It is true
that many Jews have had remarkable
careers in the learned world. The moment
the opportunity was granted them, they
grasped it with avidity, and ere long they
became brilliant students. This, too,
strange as it may appear, was a result of
the Ghetto existence. For centuries the
Jewish mind had been confined to the study
of the Jewish writings, and been sharpened in the fencing school of rabbinical
dialectics. The schools outside of the
Ghetto were closed to them. The classics
and the sciences were unknown worlds.
As soon as the open sesame of emancipation
sounded, and the doors of the schools
swung back to admit the Jew, he entered
a new domain. His mind was as a field

long fallow ; it had been gathering strength
for centuries. The learned words of pro-
fessors and of books fell upon this new
soil, and took deep root. This, together
with the keenness and acumen resulting
from the discussions in the Talmudical
schools, readily explains why he forged
ahead so rapidly.

His striking success may be traced to
another cause. If history has an example
of the "survival of the fittest" to present,
it is this of the Jews. To have survived in
spite of all the dangers and persecutions
which they encountered, is evidence sufficient that there were present among these
people the moral and mental qualities
that can successfully withstand physical
ill and harm. The fittest of the sur-
vivors, hence the choicest from out a
choice band, selected university and
professional careers. They were the products of the endurance of centuries. All
these things combined offer full explanation of a seeming anomaly.

Hard as this life in the Ghetto was, un-
bearable as it became at times, sad as

was this continued exclusion, yet these very evils were productive of virtues among the devoted people. To survive despite all these disadvantages, the Jews had to be better than their surroundings, had to live on a higher moral plane. The Ten Commandments were ever respected and observed by them. The crime of murder was practically unknown even among their poorest and most ignorant classes, rampant as it may have been among others in the same circumstances. Chastity among their women was universal; the home life was a model; never was heard issuing from a Jewish home the wail of the wife beaten by a drunken husband. A cheerful, trustful piety that illuminated the most squalid existence, and made its inhabitants content with their lot, was characteristic of the Ghetto. It was not for them to murmur against the decrees of God. He knew best, their release would come, if not in this world, then in the next. And these same qualities mark the inhabitants of the lowly, poverty-stricken quarters in our great cities,

so like the old Ghetto in all particulars
save that residence in them is voluntary,
not compulsory.

Upon modern Ghettos, the Jewish quarters in the large cities of the world, I have
hardly touched, since they do not lie
within the scope of these investigations,
but I must briefly refer to them since they
are another direct result of the officially
instituted Ghetto of the Middle Ages.
The poverty-stricken huddle together in
these districts, because here they find
companionship and sympathy, and their
social instinct is satisfied. But at least,
they are not forced to stay there, and as
soon as they desire they can remove thence.
If such a thing as a Jewish question in any
but the religious signification of the term
can be spoken of in this country, it is in
reference to these Jewish quarters in New
York and other large cities, and their inhabitants. How to break these up and
disperse their denizens over the surface of
this broad, fair land, and make them self-
supporting, self-respecting citizens, is the
great problem now pressing for solution.

There are not more than several hundred thousand all told, crowded together in three or four localities. This seems to be a large number, but scattered among the population of this vast land it is but as a drop in the ocean. These voluntary Ghettos are a constant menace, for they arouse the worst passions of non-Jewish demagogues, and the Jews are referred to as a class, and discriminated against as a separate body. The Jewish immigrant coming from the Russian Ghetto naturally drifts into this new Ghetto, and continues in the old life, for he finds much the same conditions. These last visible vestiges of Ghetto existence must be wiped out. They are fraught with menace. Charitable and philanthropic effort must be directed to this work. Millions are spent yearly to relieve the poor of these districts, but there will be no permanent relief until these Ghettos shall be no more, until these wretched immigrants will be taken in hand upon their arrival, prevented from invading the already overcrowded districts, and sent to smaller communities, there to as-

similate themselves with their American
surroundings; those already dwelling in
these sections and applying for relief must
be taken charge of by our charitable agen-
cies, and removed into more wholesome
quarters. This is a duty that devolves upon
all who seek to improve the economic and
social condition of the masses. Systematic,
intelligent, united effort alone will be
able to grapple with this hydra-headed
evil. There is no duty more imperative
than the relief of the congestion of the
slums, both in the interest of their inhabitants and of our American institutions.
The work can be begun none too soon.
The axe of improvement can be applied
to the cutting down of the tenements none
too vigorously. Every day of delay but
aggravates the evil. Away with these
Ghettos, too. The law cannot order their
removal as it did with the officially instituted Ghetto. Voluntary effort alone
will accomplish it. In the words of the
old prayer, "may we see it done quickly
in our days."

CHAPTER IX.

THE GHETTO IN LITERATURE.

Although the actual, enforced Ghetto, with the one exception of "the Pale of Settlement" in Russia, has disappeared from the face of Europe, yet the Ghetto life of Jews has found a permanent place in literature, inasmuch as during this century numerous writers have arisen who have drawn their material for most interesting tales and character sketches from the Ghetto. The life there was unique. Certain types of character were formed, and the development of personality proceeded along peculiar lines, so that this Jewish life became the legitimate object of treatment by poets and novelists. And Jewish life and Jewish characteristics, as developed in the Ghetto, are the only rightful objects of treatment in fiction portraying the Jew All other representations of the Jew as differing from other

men in aught but his religion are misrep-
resentations, and false to the real thought
and present status of the Jew, who, in
everything but his religion, is like unto
those among whom he dwells.[139]

The Ghetto novel is unique. It trans-
ports us into a life so different from our
own that it scarce seems possible that a
comparatively short period has intervened
between our day and the time wherein the
scenes which it portrays were enacted.
It depicts real life within the Ghetto, and
shows that existence there in peaceful times
was much the same as anywhere else.
There are tales of love and marriage; of
success and failure; of heroism and self-
sacrifice. There are descriptions of phases
of life and character peculiar to the Ghetto,
written, for the most part, by men whose
youthful years were passed there, and who
knew from experience the scenes which
they depicted. These stories are the swan
song of the Ghetto. They cast the gla-
mour of poetry over it, and are the one
fair product left to mankind from the dark
record of centuries.

The first to attempt a Ghetto novel was the great poet Heinrich Heine in his fragment, *Der Rabbi von Bacharach*, perhaps the finest of his prose writings. He describes the terrible experience of a rabbi of Bacharach and his wife in the fifteenth century, who, during the celebration of the *Seder*, the family festival on the eve of the Passover feast, noticed the corpse of a child that had been placed beneath their table. Knowing that the enemies of the Jews had done this to trump up the old accusation that the Jews use Christian blood on the Passover, they fled in terror of what would take place. Of this oft repeated lie, Heine says : " Another accusation which cost the Jews much blood and fear throughout the Middle Ages up to the beginning of the last century was the silly story reiterated with disgusting frequency in legends and chronicles, that the Jews stole consecrated wafers, which they pierced with knives till the blood flowed, and that they killed Christian children on their Passover in order to use the blood at their evening service. The

Jews, thoroughly hated because of their faith, their wealth, and their account books, on that holiday were completely in the hands of their enemies, who could accomplish their ruin but too easily, if they spread the report of a child-murder, or succeeded in smuggling a child's bloody corpse into the house of a Jew, and fell upon the Jewish family at night during the service. Then there was murder, plunder, and baptism, and great miracles occurred through the agency of the dead child, which the church finally even canonized." Heine describes the Frankfort Ghetto, to which the rabbi fled from the wrath to come. The oft-quoted description of Jewish female beauty that he gives in speaking of Sarah, the rabbi's wife, is worth repeating : " Her face was touchingly beautiful, even as, in general, the beauty of Jewesses is strangely touching. The consciousness of the deep misery, the bitter disgrace, and the evil experiences under which their relatives and friends live spreads over their lovely features a certain expression of suffering and watchful anxiety, which exercises a peculiar charm upon us."

Turning from Heine's fragment, we find that a number of authors have presented these *genre* pictures of Ghetto life to the reading world. Auerbach's novels, *Spinoza* and *Dichter und Kaufmann*, although concerned with Jewish subjects, can scarcely be included in this branch of literature. The versatile Aaron Bernstein, a scientist, editor, and brilliant scholar generally, wrote two novels, *Mendel Gibbor*, *i. e.* "Mendel the Strong," and *Vögele der Maggid*, *i. e.* "Vögele the Preacher," both of which portray in bright flashes and genial style that peculiar life whereof we speak. In reprinting *Vögele der Maggid* in his magazine, *Der Sinai*, in 1861, the great Jewish preacher and writer, Dr. David Einhorn, prefaced the publication with the following note: "The readers of the *Sinai* will certainly thank us for republishing this excellent novel of the brilliant Bernstein. It is permeated with the real Jewish spirit, and portrays in masterly touches phases of life and thought that have well nigh disappeared, and sound almost legendary to the younger generation. It is arousing the greatest attention in Jewish circles in Germany. Only a genial man like Bernstein, prominent as theologian as well as scientist (his work on natural history is now being reprinted in America), could write such a novel."[140]

I will quote a few passages from these tales of Bernstein. In speaking of the persecutions, he says : "The history of the legislation of all states concerning Jews, whether dictated by religious hatred or perverted benevolence, contained the source of eternal pain; this lent an ever renewed significance to the oldest prophetical lamentations." The implicit trust in God that characterized Jews even in the darkest days is well expressed thus : "Dost thou not know that with Him there is help? Is it not written, hope in God and trust in Him, for He will bring it to pass? Yes, even though thou canst not speak with man, speak to Him, and thou wilt see. His help will come." The love of the Jewish husband

15

for his wife, the foundation whereon rests
the home life of Jews, ever so highly
appreciated and praised, is well expressed
in a sympathetic reminiscence of the quiet
Salme, in *Mendel Gibbor.* " Four years
God, blessed be He, permitted us to be
together. His holy will did not bless us
with children, but her heart grew more
pious and joyful from day to day, and when
she implored God for His mercy and com-
passion, it was only her eyes that expressed
prayer to Him on high, but her lips smiled
upon her happy husband. Light rested on
her face and in her soul, until her time
came, and she was called away by God.
* * * God, blessed be He, is my witness, I did not murmur, for I lived with
my pious Yütte four years, two months,
and six days, and that was more than a
whole life and a long life." In this novel
he tells the story of the Polish Jew, Saul
Wahl, who is said to have been king of
Poland for one day during an interreg-
num.

The man entitled above all others to
the designation, " Poet of the Ghetto,"

is Leopold Kompert. Born in the Ghetto
of Münchengratz, Bohemia, in 1822, acquainted with the true life of the Ghetto
from his very infancy, he knew from experience all its phases and all the peculiar
characters developed by it. His was a
poetic soul, and he threw the glow of
ideality over Ghetto scenes, yet presented
them garbed in the elements of truth. In
a series of tales he has preserved for
later generations the peculiarities of that
life. So charmingly did he write, so new
and striking was the matter of his produc-
tions, that his tales created a great sensation in the literary world, arousing as much
attention, it is said, as Auerbach's equally
unique *Schwarzwälder Dorfgeschichten.*
These Ghetto novels of Kompert have
become part and parcel of the world's
literature. They were a revelation.
They pointed to a life unknown to the
world. Joy and sorrow, happiness and
woe, love and marriage, scenes of sickness and death, all the common happenings that go to make up daily life, are
described by him with a sympathetic feel-

ing that only a loving spirit can experience.
They are homely scenes that he pictures.
Nothing grandiose or heroic in the sense
of the uncommon appears upon his pages,
and for this very reason, because all his
stories are concerned with scenes and incidents with which every one is familiar, and
which appeal to the human heart, he exercised such power with his pen, and made
the better side of Ghetto life immortal.
Scenes of home, scenes of the heart, of
mother's love, of father's self-sacrifice, of
filial devotion, of conjugal constancy, these
form the burden of his tales, and as long as
man is interesting to man, so long must
stories of this kind meet with a sympathetic
reception. The qualities of the heart as
appearing in the Ghetto formed the inspiration of his muse, and the human heart re-
sponds to what is true or loving, wherever
it may appear. Then, too, he presented
in strong colors the strange characters peculiar to the Ghetto, the products of centuries of seclusion and exclusion, such as
the *Min*, the silent man; the *Seelenfän-
gerin*, the woman who took God's place

in protecting the helpless ; the *Dorfgeher*, the peddler ; the *Shlemihl*, the awkward individual unfortunate in every undertaking. Institutions peculiar to the Ghetto were explained to the world, such as the *Beschau*, the custom of the young men of the Ghetto to visit, with the purpose of taking to wife, the girl recommended to them by the marriage broker, or *Shadchen*. *Ohne Bewilligung* is the story of the couples who, because of the inhuman regulation limiting Jewish families to a certain number, could not obtain permission from the government to marry, and therefore, although united by a religious ceremony, were in the eyes of the law not legally married. These scenes and characters he paints with the brush of the artist, and in a manner so vivid that we perceive at once that he is writing from knowledge and with sympathy. It is only the fairer side that he presents, the horrors of that existence he passes by. He throws the shimmer of beauty over everything that he touches, and in the light of his writings the poetry of the Ghetto alone appears. Even his characters are for the most part good, and we are led to think that the darker traits that deface human nature did not exist there. This was due to his idealistic, artistic temperament. After his death, in 1886, Karl Emil Franzos, another novelist of the Ghetto, wrote of this feature of Kompert's stories : "Jewish life, as portrayed by Kompert, appears more edifying than it really is. Not that he exaggerated its good traits, or avoided the shadows and the reverse of the medal, but he did not describe these so vigorously and minutely as its bright side. This was the result, not of carefully planned purpose on his part, but of his artistic individuality and character. He could not speak a harsh word, or express an adverse opinion. Wickedness was to him a source of spiritual pain, and, in art, he hated to analyze a low character." This is a fault of omission, but the purity and ideality of Kompert's writings atone for a defect of this kind, a defect readily pardoned. Professor H. Steinthal most beautifully says : " What was it that guided Kompert's pen ?

Gratitude, and the love of a Jewish son
for his Jewish mother, the Ghetto street;
for this revealed to him the place of his
childhood, full of the brightest sunlight.
His glance was not directed to the narrowness of the street or the pavement;
he preferred to look up to the sky from
which brightness beamed."

Now let us examine more closely the
stories, so distinctive in their treatment,
which fascinated the reading world.

Kompert wrote his first stories of the
Ghetto in 1846—1847 for the Vienna *Jahr-
buch für Israeliten.* Then followed in
rapid succession his many other tales, "At
the Plough," a lengthy romance, " Bohemian Jews," "New Stories from the
Ghetto," " Tales of a Jews' Street," volumes of short stories, and " Amongst
Ruins." These comprise his Jewish stories;
he wrote others also, but with them we are
not concerned here.

First, a few words as to what Ghetto
life itself was to him. He says in one of
his stories: "In the Ghetto every individual is bound by a thousand chains to

the community. Woe has here a thousand tongues, and if the lightning blast
the happiness of a single one, a thousand eyelashes are cast down."[141]

Of the inhabitants of the Ghetto, he
tells us: "They had their sorrows and
troubles, as we have ours, and when misfortune came upon them, it visited them
with harsh and heavy blows. Rude and
unfeeling, it struck them with doubled
fist. But when their hearts expanded
with happiness, and they wished to enjoy
themselves, they were like such as swim
in refreshing waters. They plunged in,
fresh and courageous, and permitted themselves to be carried by the stream whithersoever it, not they, wished."[142] Again:
" We must not look for much romance, for
we are in the Ghetto, and there the people
have something else to do besides standing idly at the wells and helping beautiful
Rachels remove heavy stones. The people
there are themselves stones, and must
permit themselves to be shoved and moved
by the caprice of others."[143]

He wrote in the purest German; he

never uses the jargon except when it serves to bring out his characters in stronger light. His stories are truly poetic and artistic.

In his tale, *Die Jahrzeit*,[144] *i. e.*, the anniversary of a parent's death, always commemorated by the children throughout their lives by the *Kaddish*, that distinctively Jewish prayer, he portrays the loving attachment of the Jew for his dead, and the anxiety of the living to have some one say the *Kaddish* for them, when they have passed away. An abstract of this tale will furnish a good example of Kompert's power and style. The story tells of Jacob Löw, a rich man, who had five promising sons and one daughter. He is delighted with the thought that there will be five sons to survive him and recite the *Kaddish* for the parents after their death. His hopes, however, are shattered, for, one after another, these sons succumb to a treacherous disease. All his expectations now center in the daughter; if there is to be anyone to remember him after death, it will be her children. He lavishes every-

thing upon her. She is a gay, careless
child, and falls in love with a certain Jac-
ques. Her parents oppose the match.
The father had set his heart upon her
marrying his cousin Maier, a good-hearted
though homely young man. She, however, marries the man of her choice, and
follows him to Hungary. Her father dis-
cards her ; the mother dies ; the father
grows morose, hard, sullen. There is no
one to remember the *Jahrzeit* of his wife
except himself. He is an old man ; when
he dies there will be no one to recite the
Kaddish ; both will be forgotten. Mean-
while the daughter fares badly ; she has
married unhappily ; her husband deserts
her, and goes ·to America. She returns
to her home, and passes the night on a
bench in front of her father's house,
her little boy beside her. Early in the
morning, before anyone is astir in the
street, her cousin Maier, who happens to
have left his house, comes across her, and
shocked at her appearance and her homeless condition, induces her to go into his
home to his parents, her relatives. A

happy idea strikes him by which to effect
a reconciliation with the father. It is two
days before the anniversary of the mother's death. By dint of hard work and
perseverance he succeeds in teaching the
child the *Kaddish.* On the anniversary
he takes the child to the synagogue. The
close of the story had best be told in
Kompert's own words : " The decisive
moment had come. Maier took up the
boy quickly, and carried him through the
rows of worshippers up to Jacob Löw, at
whose side he placed him. Lost in the
painful recollection of what the prayer
aroused in this hour, Jacob looked straight
before him, and did not notice what was
taking place round about.

He began the prayer. * * * But clearer
and ever clearer resounded the same words
from the mouth of a child at his side. His
eyes involuntarily filled with tears. * * *
He paused and listened, and let the child
speak alone. * * * All his woe, all the icy
pain at his heart, which had chilled him
for so many years, melted before these
pure, clear, childish sounds. That

which he had always concealed in his innermost heart, the longing for his lost daughter, the secret which he thought no human soul would ever discover, this child unraveled. * * * 'Who is this child?' he cried with piercing voice, when the last words of the prayer had scarcely sounded. 'Cousin,' said Maier behind him, * * * 'it is your and Esther's grandchild. * * * It is Blümele's child.'

With a faint cry Jacob Löw staggered backwards, and would have sustained a severe fall had Maier not caught him in his arms. His face was deathly pale, he had fainted.

A great commotion arose among the worshippers; they crowded around; an unheard of thing had taken place before their eyes.

All at once Jacob Löw stood up supported by Maier. He began to weep bitterly.

'Where is the child?' cried he, not noticing it on account of his streaming tears. 'Where is Blümele's child?'

Then Maier picked up the boy, and laid

him upon his grandfather's breast. Trembling arms embraced the child. * * *

'Blümele! Where is my Blümele!'
cried Jacob Löw.

So the prayer of a child had reconciled
father and daughter."

Blümele's husband died in America;
she married her cousin, and Jacob Löw
lived to see many grandchildren, who
would recite the *Kaddish* for him after his
death.

Of the *Kaddish*, that remarkable prayer,
which even to-day the most lax and in-
different Jew feels it his duty to recite,
as an act of filial piety, in memory of a
deceased parent, Kompert says:

"The *Kaddish* is that peculiar prayer
handed down from generation to generation, from century to century, which, spoken
in the language of ancient Zion, forms
an essential portion of the daily service.
Its origin is mysterious; angels are said
to have brought it down from heaven and
taught it to men. About this prayer the
tenderest threads of filial feeling and
human recollection are entwined; for it

is the prayer of the orphans! When the father or the mother dies, the surviving sons are to recite it twice daily, morning and evening, throughout the year of mourning, and then also on each recurring anniversary of the death, or, as it is called in the Ghetto, on the *Jahrzeit*, for it possesses wonderful power. * * *

Truly, if there is any bond strong and indissoluble enough to chain heaven to earth it is this prayer! It keeps the living together, and forms the bridge to the mysterious realm of the dead. One might almost say that this prayer is the watchman and the guardian of the people by whom alone it is uttered; therein lies the warrant of its continuance. Can a people disappear and be annihilated * * * so long as a child remembers its parents? * * * It may sound strange : in the midst of the wildest dissipation has this prayer of recollection recalled to his better self many a dissolute character, so that he has bethought himself, and for a short time at least purified himself by honoring the memory of his parents. Such a one may

well shudder when he thinks of the life
he has led, and compares it with that
which he might have passed, if the eye of
father and mother had still watched over
him !

Because this prayer is a resurrection in
the spirit of the perishable in man, because
it does not acknowledge death, because it
permits the blossom, which, withered, has
fallen from the tree of mankind, to flower
and develop again in the human heart,
therefore it possesses sanctifying power !
To know that thou wilt die, wilt pass
from this ever restless, corruptible form
into a mysterious hereafter, but that the
earth dully falling on thy head will not
cover thee entirely; that there remain
those behind who know that thou hast
died, who, wherever they may be on this
wide earth, whether they be poor or rich,
will send this prayer after thee; to know
that thou canst call no green spot in this
world thine, that thou leavest them no
house, no estate, no field by which they
must remember thee, and that yet they
will cherish thy memory as their dearest

inheritance ; * * * insignificant, despised, a bubble though thou wast in life, they raise thee to importance long after thou art no longer here ; * * * who is there that cannot comprehend Jacob Löw's peculiar train of thought, and that he found great satisfaction in the knowledge that five boys would say *Kaddish* for him ?"

Plain, homely scenes, occurrences in daily life, the old and ever new story of love and devotion, as developed among the Jews, he beautifully describes. The "Jewish heart" that beats so kindly and sympathetically, that even in greatest misfortune retained its interest in men, he knew how to appreciate. In one place, in speaking of this term, "Jewish heart," he says : "This word embodies something inexpressible, and it is difficult to make it even approximately understood. What may appear to some an empty sound takes on a reality of which the Ghetto is best able to speak. This 'heart' is an historical tradition—whoever appeals to it, desires to say, 'Do not forget! be mind-

ful of that which your fathers, my fathers,
suffered together, what they experienced,
how they rejoiced, and also sorrowed !' It
is the expression of the strongest fellowship, the secret bond of sympathy in a
brother's fate * * * whatever the Ghetto
is, and however it may appear, without
that 'heart' it would be something entirely different. In all likelihood, we
would have nothing to report about it !"[145]
" The Jew can give to all, the Jew does
not hesitate, and that is the case because
the Jew has a heart."

And who will not appreciate these words?
"A mother's heart is a peculiar thing.
Stronger and more courageous than any
hero in battle, if it is necessary to defend
a child, whether from real danger or
from the slightest fancied evil, it becomes fearful, almost cowardly, when it
anticipates danger."[146] Throughout his
writings occur these beautiful expressions,
giving proof of his deep and searching insight into human nature.

But Kompert was more than the poet
of the feelings. He was enthusiastically

16

interested in the complete emancipation
of the Jew from the oppression of centuries.
All plans to further the development of
trades among Jews found his hearty support, and in one of his stories, *Trenderl,*[147]
he tells of a Jewish boy who became a
skilled workman.   He felt that, more than
anything else, the Jew's working in the
same trades with others, a privilege that
past legislation had denied him, would tend
to break down the barriers of prejudice,
and so he exclaims, " Hammer away, O,
locksmith ! every blow on the anvil breaks
a link from the chain of slavery that binds
thy people, and sounds a welcome to the
new time coming."

In the movement to make Jews farmers
he showed lively interest.   He felt that
the Jew must out from the Ghetto with
its trading into the field with its freedom.
The day of emancipation that had dawned
must see more and more Jews ploughing
the fields and harvesting the grain.   The
farmer is a free man, he says, far, far superior to the trader and the merchant.   His
beautiful story, " The Princess,"[148] dwells

on the superiority, the independence of the farmer's life, and describes the doings and the happiness of the Jewish agriculturist. He makes his farmer say: "Can you not be made to understand that in this day of ours a farmer counts for far more than all who sit in their shops, and contend with one another for customers? * * * I, who dwell here on my estate, and owe no man a penny, I am more than the people in the 'Streets' with all their money and treasures." In his romance, "At the Plough," he treats of the same subject. He tells of a family that left the Ghetto, and took to farming. The book teaches a like lesson of the departure of the Jews from the Ghetto, the participation in the new life that a kindlier legislation opened to Jews, the struggle to give up the old familiar habits, and the final adaptation to new conditions. These stories he wrote *con amore.* He was a lover of nature, and his descriptions of the fields and their products are masterly. He felt that a new and better time had come, that the Jews would have to adapt themselves to new conditions, that the Ghetto with its narrowing influences would have to give way to the larger life of nature and companionship with men in general.

Although he so poetically portrayed the scenes and the life of the Ghetto, yet was he a child of his age. He was much affected and influenced by the new spirit. In writing his stories of the Ghetto, he seemed to be describing incidents of a distant past; in his tales depicting the struggles in adopting new ideas and new occupations, he stood in the present. The story that gives most complete expression to the new spirit is his longest tale, "Amongst Ruins." Here the new struggles with the old, the letter with the spirit. Tolerance between Jew and Christian is the text; a new life arising from the ruins of what was wrong, intolerant, hateful in the old. Thus was Leopold Kompert a power; he opened a new department in literature. He moved in a narrow groove, it may be said, but on that very account he reached such mastery in his art. He has had followers and imitators, but as the interpreter of the now vanished life of the Ghetto he stands unequalled.

There have been many others who, after Kompert had given the impulse, worked the mine of Ghetto life, and wrote stories more or less true to life. We may mention S. Kohn, author of *Gabriel*, and many other stories, whose scenes are laid in the Ghetto of Prague ; Edward Kulke, E. O. Tauber, Michael Klapp, S. H. Mosenthal, Leo Herzberg-Fränkel, Fanny Lewald, S. Formstecher, Ludwig Philippson, M. Lehmann, Max Ring, M. Goldschmidt;[149] Ludwig August Frankl, who wove the legends of the Prague Ghetto into his poem, *Der Primator ;* Phoebus Philippson, in his strange and powerful tale, *Der unbekannte Rabbi ;* Nathan Samuely, author of " Pictures of Jewish Life in Galicia," and many others. There are several living authors who should be particularly mentioned as excelling in the treatment of Ghetto life. Karl Emil Franzos may be called the intellectual scion of Kompert. His scenes are for the most part laid in Galicia and the Bukowina. He depicts the darker and sadder sides of Ghetto life. He is different from Kompert in this. Kompert's was an optimistic nature ; he lived in the period of emancipation when hope gilded the horizon. Franzos, living in a later day, has experienced the futility of those hopes. The Jews of the Galician towns are as they were before the year 1848, which promised to bring about an entire revolution in the status of Jews everywhere in Europe. His best known Jewish writings are, "The Jews of Barnow" and "From the Don to the Danube," sketches that inform the world of the characteristics of Jewish life in those far-off and unknown quarters of Galicia, where superstition is rife, and firm belief in the miracles wrought by the wonder-rabbi of Sadagora rules. It is a pity that Franzos paints only the sombre pictures, but the misery and sorrows of that life seem to have so impressed themselves upon his mind as to force out of sight the brighter and lighter scenes. His last Ghetto novel, *Judith Trachtenberg*, is a powerful

tale, and treats the vexed subject of intercourse betwen Christians and Jews. The
moral he desires to teach is the impos-
sibility of happiness in mixed marriages.
Judith Trachtenberg is the victim of the
unhappiness caused by such a union. Her
father says to her at the start, fire and
water will not readily mix. In the intoxi-
cation of love she consents to become a
Christian. When she learns that she has
been duped, a revulsion of feeling sets in.
She desires to remain a Jewess ; her husband, a Christian nobleman, looks down
upon Jews ; she feels that there is only
misery in store for them both, and
rather than live on so, she determines to
die after having exacted a promise that
she will be buried as a Jewess. It is better for her, better for her husband. As a
Jewess she was content ; she can never be
anything else. A home disrupted by religion must be unhappy. The author sets
forth the consequences of intermarriage
in these strong colors to make the lesson
as powerful as possible.

I mention further the well known

writer, Sacher-Masoch, who, although a Christian, has written many realistic stories of Jewish life in Poland and Galicia.

Born in Lemberg, he is thoroughly well acquainted with the scenes which he describes and the life which he portrays. He is altogether unprejudiced, and although his tales do not always place his characters in the most favorable light, yet we feel that he is true to nature.

Some years ago, a new writer of Ghetto novels, Miss E. P. Orzeszko, appeared on the horizon, and created a sensation with her book *Meier Esofowicz*.[50] The scene is laid in the far off village of Szybow, Russia, and depicts the struggles of a youth whose desire for culture stirred up all the bitter fanaticism of the strict Jewish conformists. It is the tale of the struggle of enlightenment with ignorance, of reason with blind faith, of the spirit of religion with the form. Meier represents all the strivings of a lofty human soul for the best and noblest, rising above outward circumstances and surroundings; his enemies embody the uncompromising fealty to tradition. The scenes are powerfully drawn. The story is essentially one of to-day, and the author has well succeeded in depicting the different currents of religious thought. Since then Miss Orzeszko has written other Jewish stories, one of which, " A Flower," has lately appeared in the columns of the *Allgemeine Zeitung des Judenthums.*[151]

The latest writer of sketches of Ghetto life, and at the same time the first English author of strength to undertake the treatment of the traits developed in the confines of Jewry, is Israel Zangwill, whose book entitled "The Children of the Ghetto" appeared recently. It is true that his sketches are pictures of life in the Jewish quarter of London, which is not a Ghetto in the sense in which I have considered Ghettos. This Jewish quarter was the domicile voluntarily chosen by Jews who settled in the great city, and, therefore, this book scarcely comes within the range of my subject, but the traits and characteristics developed in this quarter, as set forth in the pages of his volumes, are much the same as the Ghetto everywhere produced. The inhabitants came for the most part from real Ghettos, and transferred to their new home the peculiarities acquired in the old. These sketches are unique, different from what we had grown accustomed to in the Ghetto novels of the German writers mentioned. The author writes of present conditions, and throws many a flash-light of keen observation upon modern English Jewish life in the east and west ends of London. The small vices and the many virtues of the children of the Ghetto are skilfully set forth in these powerful sketches, unlike any thing in English literature.

My task is done. I have traced the establishment of the Ghetto from its beginning to the day of its removal in civilized lands, and have presented its life in its various phases and localities. It is a long, sad story of religious repression and sectarian hatred, and forms a gloomy chapter in the volume of the dark doings of men. The Jew, however, bears no rancor ; he thanks God that this is past, and with the optimism characteristic of his religion

works on and hopes on, looking forward
to the coming of the time when all men
will be free to think, free to act, free to
live anywhere and everywhere on the earth,
which "God has given to the children of
men."

NOTES AND INDEX

NOTES.

[1] Frederic Heidekoper, Judaism at Rome, B. C. 76 to A. D. 140, p. 6. New York, 1876.

[2] Josephus, Antiquities of the Jews, XIV, 4, 5. H. Graetz, Geschichte der Juden, Vol. III, p. 142. Leipsic, 1863.

E. Renan maintains that there were Jews in Rome as early as the second century B. C. E. Histoire du Peuple Israël, Vol. V, p. 6. Paris, 1893.

[3] G. B. Depping, Les Juifs dans le Moyen Age, pp. 1-2. Paris, 1834.

I. Bédarride, Les Juifs en France, en Italie et en Espagne, p. 25. Paris, 1861.

[4] Romans, XV, 24.

[5] *Ibid* , 28.

[6] " Haeretici, si se transferre noluerint ad ecclesiam catholicam, nec ipsis catholicas dandas esse puellas : sed neque Judaeis, neque haereticis dare placuit ; eo quod nulla possit esse societas fideli cum infideli. Si contra interdictum fecerint parentes abstineri per quinquennium placet." See Labbe et Cosartii, Concilia Sacrosancta, Vol. I, pp. 1273-1276. Paris, 1671-1672 ; also, Conciliarum omnium generalium et provincialium collectio regia, Vol. I, p. 645. Paris, 1644.

[7] "Si vero quis clericus vel fidelis cum Judaeis cibum sumpserit, placuit cum a communione abstinere, ut debeat emendari." *Ibid.*, p. 651.

[8] "Admoneri placuit possessores, ut non patiantur fructus suos quos a Deo percipiunt, a Judaeis benedici : ne

(255)

nostram irritam et infirmam faciant benedictionem. Si quis post interdictum facere usurpaverit, penitus ab ecclesia abjiciatur." *Ibid.*

[9] Graetz, Geschichte der Juden, Vol. V, pp. 55-56.

[10] Depping, Les Juifs dans le Moyen Age, p. 4.

[11] Martin Bouquet, Recueil des Historiens des Gaules, Vol. I, p. 746. Paris, 1840-1876.

[12] Graetz, Geschichte der Juden, Vol. V, p. 219.

Otto Stobbe, Die Juden in Deutschland während des Mittelalters, p. 201. Brunswick, 1866. See also the article, "Stammen die Juden in den südlichen Rheinlanden von den Vangionen ab?" in Brüll's *Jahrbücher für jüdische Geschichte und Literatur*, Vol. IV, pp. 34-40. Frankfort-on-the-Main, 1879.

[13] Stobbe, Die Juden in Deutschland, p. 88.

[14] *Ibid.*, p. 200, note 10.

[15] Moritz Stern, Aus der älteren Geschichte der Juden in Regensburg, in *Zeitschrift für die Geschichte der Juden in Deutschland*, Vol. I, p. 383.

[16] Stobbe, Die Juden in Deutschland, p. 200, note 10

[17] Hugo Barbeck, Geschichte der Juden in Nürnberg und Fürth, p. 6. Nuremberg, 1878.

[18] On the subject of the earliest notices concerning Jews in England, see Joseph Jacobs, The Jews of Angevin England, p. IX and pp. 2-3. New York and London, 1893.

[19] Salomon Goldschmidt, Geschichte der Juden in England, pp. 2-4. Berlin, 1886.

[20] For first settlement in Bohemia, see below, p. 84.

[21] Graetz, Geschichte der Juden, Vol. VI, p. 269.

[22] Stobbe, Die Juden in Deutschland, p. 12.

[23] For the relation between the king and the Jews in England, see Jacobs, The Jews of Angevin England. Introduction, p. XV ff.

[24] Stobbe, Geschichte der Juden in Deutschland, p. 19.

[25] For instance, in the act of Frederick I, of the year

1156, by which Margrave Henry was created duke of Austria, among other privileges granted him is this of having Jews in his land : "et potest in terris suis omnibus tenere Judaeos, " etc. See *Sulamith,* Vol. IV, p. 220.

[26] "Pestmässige Abschliessung," Leopold Zunz, Die gottesdienstlichen Vorträge der Juden, p. 451. Frankfort-on-the-Main, 1892.

[27] David Kaufmann, Don Joseph Nassi, der Begründer der Colonien im Heiligen Lande und die Gemeinde von Cori in der Campagna, in *Allgemeine Zeitung des Judenthums,* Vol. XLIX, p. 9.

[28] See below, pp. 35-39.

[29] Stobbe, Die Juden in Deutschland, p. 176.

Höniger, Zur Geschichte der Juden im früheren Mittelalter, in *Zeitschrift für die Geschichte der Juden in Deutschland,* Vol. I, p. 90.

[30] Leopold Treitel, Ghetto und Ghetto Dichter, p. 7, in M. Brann's Volks und Haus Kalender. Breslau, 1892.

[31] A. Berliner, Aus den letzten Tagen des römischen Ghetto, p. 2. Berlin, 1886.

Joseph Jacobs, Studies in Jewish Statistics, Appendix, p. XXI, note 3. London, 1891.

[32] E. Rodocanachi, Le Saint-Siége et les Juifs, p. 41, note 4. Paris, 1891.

[33] For an account of the Portuguese Judiarias, see M. Kayserling, Juden in Portugal, pp. 49-52. Leipsic, 1867.

[34] Graetz, Geschichte der Juden, Vol. IX, p. 46.

[35] See below, Chap. V.

[36] Bédarride, Les Juifs in France, en Italie et en Espagne, p. 335.

[37] *Ibid.,* p. 365.

[38] Graetz, Geschichte der Juden, Vol. X, p. 49.

[39] L. Erler, Historisch-kritische Uebersicht der national-ökonomischen und social-politischen Literatur, p. 372. Mayence, 1879.

[40] *Ibid.,* p. 50.

17

⁴¹ L. Zunz, Zur Geschichte und Literatur, p. 488. Berlin, 1845.

⁴² *Ibid.*, p. 505.

⁴³ *Ibid.*, p. 491.

⁴⁴ *Ibid.*, p. 500.

⁴⁵ *Ibid.*, p. 514.

⁴⁶ Höniger, Zur Geschichte der Juden im früheren Mittelalter, in *Zeitschrift für die Geschichte der Juden in Deutschland*, Vol. I, p. 91.

⁴⁷ Stobbe, Die Juden in Deutschland, p. 94.

⁴⁸ Moritz Stern, Aus der älteren Geschichte der Juden in Regensburg, in *Zeitschrift für die Geschichte der Juden in Deutschland*, Vol. I, p. 383.

⁴⁹ Stobbe, Die Juden in Deutschland, p. 63.

⁵⁰ See below, Chap. IV.

⁵¹ Stobbe. Die Juden in Deutschland, p. 276.

⁵² *Allgemeine Zeitung des Judenthums*, Vol. LV (October, 1891), p. 500.

⁵³ See below, Chap. III.

⁵⁴ Berliner, Aus dem inneren Leben der deutschen Juden im Mittelalter, p. 52, quoted in *Allgemeine Zeitung des Judenthums*, Vol. LV, p. 500. See also Frankel's *Monatsschrift für die Geschichte und Wissenschaft des Judenthums*, Vol. X (1861), p. 280.

⁵⁵ "In nomine sanctae et individuae Trinitatis. Ego, Rudigerus, qui et Huozmannus cognomine, Nemetensis qualiscunque Episcopus Cum ex Spirensi villa urbem facerem, putavi melius amplificare honorem Loci nostri, si et Judaeos colligerem. Collectos igitur locavi extra communionem et habitationem caeterorum civium, et ne pejoris turbae insolentia facile turbarentur, muro eosdem circumdedi : Locum vero habitationis eorum juste acquisieram ; primo namque clivum partim pecunia, partim commutatione : Vallem autem dono cohaeredum accepi: Locum, inquam, illum tradidi eis ea conditione ut annuatim persolvant III Libras et dimidiam Spirensis

monetae ad communem usum Fratrum ; attribui etiam eis
intra ambitum habitationis suae et e regione extra usque
navalem portum et in ipso navali portu, liberam potestatem
commutandi aurum et argentum, emendi vero et vendendi
omnia quae placuerint, eandemque licentiam tradidi eis
per totam civitatem. Dedi insuper eis de praedio Eccle-
siae locum sepulturae sub haereditaria conditione. Illud
quoque addidi, si ut Judaeus aliunde apud ipsos habitatus
fuerit, nullum ibi solvat teloneum ; deinde, sicut tri-
bunus urbis inter cives, ita Archisynagogus suus omnem
judicet querimoniam quae contigerit inter eos et adversus
eos. At, si quam forte non determinare potuerit, ascendit
causa ante Episcopum civitatis, vel ejus camerarium.
Vigilias, tuiciones, municiones, circa suum tantummodo
exhibeant ambitum ; tuiciones vero communiter cum
servientibus. Nutrices et conductitios servientes ex
nostris licite habeant ; carnes mactatas, quas viderint sibi
illicitas secundum legis suae sanctionem, licite vendant
Christianis, licite emant eas Christiani. Ad summam,
pro cumulo benignitatis concessi illis legem, quancumque
meliorem habet populus Judaeorum in qualibet urbe,
Teutonici Regni.

Quam Traditionem, atque concessionem, ne aliquis
meorum successorum ejus pejorare, vel ad majorem
censum eos constringere valeat, tanquam ipsi hanc con-
ditionem sibi usurpaverint et non ab Episcopo acceperint,
hanc cartam praedictae Traditionis idoneam testis reliqui
eis. Et ut ejusdem rei memoria per temporalia saecula
permaneat, manu propria subscribendo corroboravi ac
sigilli mei impressione, ut infra videri potest insigniri
perfeci.

Data est haec carta idibus Septembris, Anno Dominicae
Incarnationis MLXXXIIII Indict VII (mediante fere
Januario) Anno XII ex quo coepit praesidere in eadem
civitate praenominatus Episcopus, cujus est caracter
iste."

Published in *Orient* 1842, p. 391.

[56] "Quum adhuc terra Polonica sit in corpore Christian-
itatis nova plantatio, ne forte eo facilius populus Chris-
tianus a cohabientium Judaeorum superstitionibus et
pravis moribus inficiatur . . . praecipimus, ut Judaei in
hac provincia, Gneznensi commorantes, inter Christianos
permixti non habitent, sed in aliquo sequestri loco civitatis vel villae domos suas sibi contiguas sive conjunctas
habeant, ita quod a communi habitatione Christianorum,
saepe muro vel fossato habitatio separatur."—See
Stobbe, Die Juden in Deutschland, p. 176, note.

[57] "Nec recipiantur (Judaei) alicubi ultra mensem ad
habitandum, nisi in locis in quibus habuerint synagogas."
Conciliarum omnium generalium et provincialium Collectio regia, Vol. XXVIII, p. 783.

[58] " Et quod ad habitandum alicubi ultra mensem recipi
non deberent (Judaei), nisi in locis, in quibus obtinent
synagogas. Sed quia nonnulli nescientes a vetitis abstinere, statutum salubre praefati Concilii (Ravenna III)
vilipendunt, ignorantia affectata, poena docente, poterunt
cognoscere, quam sit grave constitutiones ecclesiasticos
praeterire, ideoque sacro approbante concilio volentes
huic morbo salubriter providere, monemus omnes tam
clericos quam laicos nostrae provinciae atque statuimus,
quatenus nullus de cetero locet domos ipsis Judaeis nec
locatas dimittat, aut vendat seu quocumque colore con-
cedat, vel inhabitare permittat ultra duos menses a publi-
catione praesentis constitutionis. Qui vero contra fecerit,
ipso facto excommunicationis incurrat sententiam, a qua
absolvi non possit, nisi plene satisfecerit in praedictis."
—*Ibid.*, Vol. XXIX, p. 47.

[59] " Statuimus ut Judaei et Saraceni inter Christianos,
vel Christiani inter Judaeos, vel Saracenos, domos, hos-
pitia seu alia receptacula in quibus habitent, nullatenus,
permittantur habere ; sed in civitatibus et locis ubi certae
limitationes sunt, eisdem Judaeis et Saracenis deputatae,
reducantur ad eas, et infra ipsas constituant habitationes

suas. Ubi vero Judaei et Saraceni praedicti ad habitandum non habuerint hujusmodi limitationes seu terminos
deputatos, limitentur et assignentur eisdem partes ali-
quae in civitatibus et locis praedictis a Christianorum
habitationibus separatae, infra quas reducant se, nec extra praedictam limitationem permittantur quomodolibet
commorari ; . . . Christiani autem, qui intra limitationem
Judaeis vel Saracenis, assignatam vel assignandam, habitare praesumpserint, si infra duos menses a die publica-
tionis praesentium factae in ecclesia cathedrali civitatis
vel diocesis ubi moram trahunt, se ad commorandum
inter Christianos reducere non curaverint. ad id per cen-
suram ecclesiasticam compellantur. Judaeis vero et Saracenis, si infra dictum terminum duorum mensium ubi
limitatio est facta, vel postquam dictae limitationes de
ordinatione et voluntate domini regis, vel cujuscunque
alterius domini ecclesiastici vel temporalis civitatis vel
loci factae fuerint, se ad easdem reducere noluerint vel
neglexerint, Christianorum communio subtrahatur."—
Ibid., Vol. XXIX, p. 171.

60 "Quorum (Judaeorum) ut evitetur nimia conversatio,
in aliquibus civitatum et oppidorum locis a Christianorum
cohabitatione separatis habitare compellantur et ab eccle-
siis longius quantum fieri potest." *Ibid.*,Vol. XIV, p 207.

61 "Vehementer autem a principibus petimus ut in
singulis civitatibus certum locum constituant ubi Judaei
separatim a Christianis habitatum conveniant. Et, si
quas proprias aedes Judaei in civitate habent, intra sex
menses eas, vere, non autem simulato contracto Christianis vendi jubeant."—*Ibid.*, Vol. XXXVI, p. 137.

62 H. Baerwald, Der alte Friedhof der israelitischen
Gemeinde zu Frankfurt-am-Main.   Frankfort-on-the
Main, 1880.

L. Lewysohn, Sechzig Epitaphien von Grabsteinen des
israelitischen Friedhofes zu Worms, p. 3.   Frankfort-on-
the-Main, 1855.

[63] See above, pp. 67–68.

[64] David Kaufmann in the introduction to S. Hock, Die Familien Prags nach den Epitaphien des alten jüdischen Friedhofs in Prag, p. 36.   Pressburg, 1892.

[65] See above, p. 72.

[66] The author of the *P'ne Yehoshuah*, a commentary on various sections of the Talmud, was Rabbi Jacob Joshua Falk, rabbi in Frankfort from 1741 to 1756 when he died. On the rabbis of Frankfort see M. Horowitz, Frankfurter Rabbinen.   Frankfort-on-the-Main, 1885.

[67] H. Baerwald, Der alte Friedhof der israelitischen Gemeinde zu Frankfurt-am-Main, p. 13.

[68] D. Podiebrad, Alterthümer der Prager Josefstadt, p. 131.   Prague, 1882.

[69] *Ibid.*, p. 132.

[70] Graetz, Geschichte der Juden, Vol. VI, p. 110.

G. Wolf, Die Juden (in the series, Die Völker Oesterreich-Boehmens), p. 7.   Vienna and Teschen, 1883.

[71] Wolf, Die Juden, p. 8.

[72] Graetz, Geschichte der Juden, Vol. VIII, p. 58. Wolf, Die Juden, p. 16.

[73] Isaak Markus Jost, Geschichte der Israeliten, Vol. VII, p. 275.   Breslau, 1820.

[74] Graetz, Geschichte der Juden, Vol. VIII, pp. 76-78. Wolf, Die Juden, p. 17.

[75] See above, pp. 62–66.

On the subject of the confiscation of Jewish books, see: A. Berliner, Censur and Confiscation hebräischer Bücher im Kirchenstaate, Berlin, 1891.   A. Kisch, Die Anklageartikel gegen den Talmud and ihre Vertheidigung durch Rabbi Jechiel ben Joseph vor Ludwig dem Heiligen in Paris, in Graetz-Frankel's *Monatsschrift für Geschichte und Wissenschaft des Judenthums*, Vol. XXIII (1874), pp. 10–18, 62–75, 123–130, 155–163, 204–212.   H. Graetz, Aktenstücke zur Confiscation der jüdischen Schriften in Frankfurt-am-Main unter Kaiser Maxi-

milian durch Pfefferkorn's Angeberei, *Ibid.*, Vol. XXIV
(1875), pp. 289-300, 337-343, 385-402. S. A. Hirsch, John
Pfefferkorn and the Battle of the Books, in *Jewish Quar-
terly Review*, Vol. IV, pp. 256-292. London, 1892.

[76] K. Lieben, Gal Ed. Grabsteininschriften des prager
israelitischen alten Friedhofs (with notes by S. Hock and
introduction by S. L. Rappoport), p. 22. Prague, 1856.
This incident forms the plot of S. Kohn's Ghetto novel,
Der Retter. See below, p. 115.

[77] Graetz, Geschichte der Juden, Vol. X, p. 29.

[78] A. Kisch, Die Prager Judenstadt während der Schlacht
am Weissen Berge. *Allgemeine Zeitung des Judenthums*,
Vol. LVI, p. 400.

[79] Jost, Geschichte der Israeliten, Vol. VIII, p. 227.
Frankel's *Monatsschrift für Geschichte und Wissenschaft
des Judenthums*, Vol. X (1861), p. 280.

[80] Graetz, Geschichte der Juden, Vol. X, p. 50.

[81] Wolf, Die Juden, p. 31.

[82] *Ibid.*, p. 37.

[83] From 1784 to 1849 the Jewish community of Prague
had a kind of special government, far from autonomous,
however, since its affairs, even in their details, were
under the supervision of the town magistrate. The
Jewish quarter remained distinct in one respect : the
funds necessary for its administration had to be raised
from among its own inhabitants. In 1849 even this distinction disappeared. The *Judenstadt* became incorporated with the rest of the city in all respects. Since then
the Jewish community has been a religious body only.
The old Jewish quarter is now known as the *Josefstadt.*
Podiebrad, Die Alterthümer der Prager Josefstadt, p. 120.

[84] Wolf, Die Juden, p. 112.

[85] *Ibid.*, p. 7, note.

In the introduction to Gal Ed mentioned above (note 76),
S. L. Rappoport proves that the stone supposed to date
from the year 606, and regarded as the oldest in the

cemetery, really belongs to the seventeenth century, pp. XXXVII-XL.

[86] Lieben, Gal Ed.

Hock, Die Familien Prags nach den Epitaphien des alten jüdischen Friedhofs in Prag.

[87] Zunz, Zur Geschichte und Literatur, p. 395.

[88] A. Berliner, Geschichte der Juden in Rom, Vol. I, pp. 5-6. Frankfort-on-the-Main, 1893.

[89] *Ibid.*, Vol. I, p. 25.

[90] *Ibid.*, Vol. I, p. 105.

[91] Rodocanachi, Le Saint-Siége et les Juifs, p. 25 ff.

[92] D. Cassel, article "Juden," in Ersch und Gruber's Allgemeine Encyclopädie (Part XXVII), p. 148.

[93] See above, p. 27.

[94] F. Gregorovius, Wanderjahre in Italien, Vol. I, pp. 103-104. Leipsic, 1876-1881.

[95] Quoted in Rodocanachi, Le Saint-Siége et les Juifs, p. 60.

[96] Berliner, Geschichte der Juden in Rom, Vol. II, Pt. II, p. 13.

[97] Rodocanachi, Le Saint-Siége et les Juifs, p. 2. So, for example, Alexander III (1159-1181) said that Jews were to be tolerated "pro sola humanitate," "on account of humanity alone," and Clement III (1187-1191), "ex vera gratia et misericordia," "from real mercy and pity."

M. Güdemann, Geschichte des Erziehungswesens und der Cultur der Juden in Italien während des Mittelalters, Vol. II, p. 76. Vienna, 1884.

[98] See on this point, Berliner, Geschichte der Juden in Rom, Vol. II, Pt. I, p. 34.

[99] Cassel, article "Juden," in Ersch und Gruber's Encyclopädie, p. 148, notes.

[100] See Ludwig August Frankl's poem, Tourist und Cicerone am Titusbogen in Rom, Ahnenbilder, p. 93. But Berliner, in his lately published work, Geschichte der Juden in Rom, Vol. I, p. 40, states that this tradition

is unknown among the Jews of Rome.

[101] Rodocanachi, Le Saint-Siége et les Juifs, p. 205 ff.

[102] Graetz, Geschichte der Juden, Vol. IX, pp 501-502.

[103] Gregorovius, Wanderjahre in Italien, Vol. I, p. 99.

[104] *Ibid.*, p. 100.

[105] Cassel, article "Juden," in Ersch und Gruber's Encyclopädie, p. 148.

Archibald Bower, History of the Popes, Vol. II, p. 464 Philadelphia, 1844-1845.

[106] Güdemann, Geschichte des Erziehungswesens und der Cultur der Juden in Italien, Vol. II, p. 77

[107] Gregorovius, Geschichte der Stadt Rom im Mittelalter vom fünften bis zum sechzehnten Jahrhundert, Vol. IV, p. 396. Stuttgart, 1869-1873.

[108] Cassel, article "Juden," in Ersch und Gruber's Encyclopädie, p. 148.

[109] Bower, History of the Popes, Vol. II, p. 464.

[110] Erler, Historisch-kritische Uebersicht der national-ökonomischen und social-politischen Literatur, p. 389.

[111] Bower, History of the Popes, Vol. II, p. 470.

[112] Berliner, Geschichte der Juden in Rom, Vol. II, p. 39.

[113] Rodocanachi, Le Saint-Siége et les Juifs, p. 284.

[114] *Ibid.*, p. 285.

[115] *Ibid.*, p. 301.

[116] *Ibid.*, p. 306.

[117] Gregorovius, Wanderjahre in Italien, Vol. I, p. 100.

[118] Before the institution of the Ghetto, there were a number of synagogues in different portions of the city. Berliner, Geschichte der Juden in Rom, Vol. II, pp. 12-13.

[119] *Ibid.*, Vol. II, p. 107.

[120] A thorough discussion of the origin and history of the blood accusation may be found in Prof. Hermann L. Strack, Der Aberglaube in der Menschheit, Blut-Morde und Blut-Ritus. Munich, 1892.

[121] In 1886. See Berliner, Aus den letzten Tagen des römischen Ghetto, p. 8.

[122] The Persecution of the Jews in Russia, p. 5. London, 1891. Report of the Russo-Jewish Committee.

[123] Leo Errera, Les Juifs Russes, Extermination ou Emancipation ? p. 18. Brussels, 1893.

These May laws were certainly inhuman, but in the spring of 1894 the special commission appointed to inquire into the Jewish question recommended to the authorities at St. Petersburg a number of provisions, compared with which the May laws of 1882 seem only a beginning. These provisions, as reported in the press, are as follows :

To forbid the Jews from residing in those places where the real estate is the property of the peasantry.

To banish from the villages of the western district all those Jews who have attained their majority since the passing of the May laws of 1882; and to forbid all Jews, as soon as they have attained their majority, from taking up their residence in villages that belong to the peasantry.

To extend to all the Polish districts those provisions of the May laws of 1882 which prohibit Jews from settling outside the towns as well as from acquiring property in land.

To enact that all those Jews who do not act in accordance with the restrictive laws concerning residence in the western provinces (districts of the Pale of Settlement and of Poland) are to be subjected to a special punishment of four months' imprisonment in addition to transport by *étape*.

To institute special supervision over those Jews who, according to the new laws, have the right to sojourn in the villages. This supervision is to be entrusted to the village police, who are to draw up complete lists of Jews coming under this category. These lists are to be kept in the government offices and to be open for general inspection, and the bureau is to have the right of expelling from the hamlets and villages any Jews who may be considered open to suspicion.

To restrict throughout the whole empire the rights of the Jews in reference to the purchase of real estate.

To revoke that law which allows Jewish mechanics, doctors and assistants, dentists, and wet-nurses to settle in all parts of the country.

To forbid the Jews from entering the provinces of the interior in order to learn pharmaceutical chemistry, medicine, and dentistry.

To expel from the districts of the interior all apothecaries, medical assistants, and wet-nurses of the Jewish religion who now reside there.

To institute a special punishment, in addition to transport by *étape*, for all those Jews who may offend against the above laws concerning sojourn in the districts of the interior.

At the time of writing, it is not known whether or not these recommendations have been adopted.

[124] The Persecution of the Jews in Russia, pp. 7-8.

[125] Harold Frederic, The New Exodus. A Study of Israel in Russia, pp. 260-261. New York, 1892.

[126] Errera, Les Juifs Russes, pp. 68-69.

[127] *Ibid.*, p. 83.

[128] Hall Caine, "Scenes on the Russian Frontier." London *Jewish Chronicle*, December 10, 1892

[129] Frederic, The New Exodus, p. 164.

[130] Nicolas de Gradowsky, La Situation Légale des Israélites en Russie, Vol. I, p. 326 ff. Paris, 1891.

[131] Frederic, The New Exodus, p. 224.

[132] The Persecution of the Jews in Russia, p. 20.

[133] Anatole Leroy Beaulieu, Les Juifs Russes et leur Ghetto, in Les Juifs de Russie, Recueil d'Articles et d' Études sur leur Situation Légale, Sociale et Économique. Paris, 1891.

[134] See Errera, Les Juifs Russes, pp. 162-177.

[135] Charles G. Leland is said to have such a work in preparation.

[136] Zunz, Die gottesdienstlichen Vorträge der Juden, pp. 453-457.

Güdemann, Geschichte des Erziehungswesens und der Cultur der Juden in Deutschland, während des vierzehnten und des fünfzehnten Jahrhunderts, p. 280 ff. Vienna, 1888.

See also an article on "The Jargon," by L. N. Dembitz in *The American Hebrew* (New York), May 6, 1892.

[137] I. Zangwill, Children of the Ghetto, Vol. I, p. 6. Philadelphia, 1892.

[138] Judaism at the World's Parliament of Religions, *passim*. Cincinnati, 1894.

[139] See the author's Jew in English Fiction, p. 8 ff. Cincinnati, 1889.

[140] David Einhorn, *Sinai*, Vol. VI, p. 186.

[141] Leopold Kompert, Gesammelte Schriften, Vol. I, p. 11. Leipsic, 1887.

[142] *Ibid.*, Vol. IV, p. 48.

[143] *Ibid.*, Vol. I, p. 246.

[144] *Ibid.*, Vol. V, pp. 1-57.

[145] *Ibid.*, Vol. V, p. 62.

[146] *Ibid.*, Vol. IV, p. 82.

[147] *Ibid.*, Vol. II, p. 220.

[148] *Ibid.*, Vol. IV, p. 202.

[149] Adolph Kohut, The Ghetto Novel and its Representatives. *The Menorah Monthly* (New York), Vol. IV, p. 351.

[150] The English translation appeared in *The Jewish Reformer* (New York). January to June, 1886.

[151] January 8 to February 5, 1892.

INDEX.

(269)

18